CHILD POVERTY AND THE CANADIAN WELFARE STATE

From Entitlement to Charity

CHILD POVERTY AND THE CANADIAN WELFARE STATE

From Entitlement to Charity

Shereen Ismael

 The University of Alberta Press

Published by

The University of Alberta Press
Ring House 2
Edmonton, Alberta, Canada T6G 2E1

Copyright © The University of Alberta Press 2006

Library and Archives Canada Cataloguing in Publication Data

Ismael, Shereen T. (Shereen Tareq)
    Child poverty and the Canadian welfare state : from entitlement
to charity / Shereen Ismael.

Includes bibliographical references and index.
ISBN 0-88864-461-2

1. Children--Canada--Social conditions. 2. Children--Services
for--Canada. 3. Poverty--Canada. 4. Canada--Social policy. 5. Welfare
state--Canada. I. Title.

HQ792.C3I86 2006   361.6′10830971   C2006-905029-5

Printed and bound in Canada.
First edition, first printing, 2006.

The University of Alberta Press is committed to protecting our natural environment. As
part of our efforts, this book is printed on stock produced by New Leaf Paper: it contains
100% post-consumer recycled fibres and is acid- and chlorine-free.

The University of Alberta Press gratefully acknowledges the support received for its
publishing program from The Canada Council for the Arts. The University of Alberta Press
also gratefully acknowledges the financial support of the Government of Canada through
the Book Publishing Industry Development Program (BPIDP) and from the Alberta
Foundation for the Arts for our publishing activities.

Canada Council   Conseil des Arts   Canadä
for the Arts   du Canada

Additional Appendix D available at:
http://www.uap.ualberta.ca/UAP.asp?lid=4
2&bookid=475

To Bibi and Jidu who parented, persevered, and persisted
with the utmost patience, kindness and wisdom.
Thank you for putting up with it for all these years.

And to my sister Jenann, selfless, kind and oh so patient.

Contents

I grew up as the Canadian welfare state matured, and like so many things we take for granted, I did not appreciate it until it was gone. Child hunger and homelessness—in my childhood considered either sorrowful reflections of an economically impoverished society or shameful reflections of a morally impoverished state—have become commonplace in my children's generation. Now it is the poor in our society who are considered morally deprived and the rich as virtuously entitled. The welfare state was born in the mid twentieth century as an instrument of social reform to make capitalism more humane. In its heyday, social policy was an instrument for mediating between the rich and the poor to reduce social injustice (exacerbated by income inequality). Thus, the trajectory of social policy development under the welfare state model was one of increasing social entitlement. But that was then. Now social policy is an instrument for increasing labour force participation. And the trajectory of social policy development has been one of reducing social entitlement and mobilizing charity.

By the end of the twentieth century, the definition of social reform had been recast to mean making capitalism more efficient. The welfare state model succumbed to the residual state model, and social policy became an instrument for reducing the constraints of child care and disability on labour force participation. Poor families, disenfranchised from social entitlements by the neo-liberal process of social policy reform, rely on food banks and community largesse to meet the basic needs of their children. Statistics indicate that from 20 to 25 percent of Canadian children are poor—that is, their families live below the poverty line. They also indicate that the depth of poverty has increased over the past decade, suggesting that the poor are getting poorer, even as the rich get richer.

This book represents my efforts to understand the changes in social policy that normalize the existence of child poverty in a rich society like Canada. To this end, I examine changes in the principles, plans and course of action of federal social policy. Taking the 1989 House of Commons Resolution to abolish child poverty by 2000 as a point of departure,

Chapter One examines principles in terms of changing state discourse around poverty. The changing plans and course of action are tracked in Chapters Two and Three, which recount the transition from entitlement to charity. Chapter Four examines the impact of changing federal policy on child poverty. In the light of these examinations, Chapter Five locates the transition from entitlement to charity in the nexus of social policy reform and the normalization of child poverty.

Acknowledgements

From the very inception of this project at the dawn of the new millennium, I have received encouragement and support. While I cannot innumerate all who have contributed to my efforts, I wish to acknowledge the institutional support I received from the University of Northern British Columbia in initiating my work on this project when I started my academic career there as an Assistant Professor in Social Work, and from the Social Science and Humanities Council of Canada Post-Doctoral Fellowship program, which provided me the opportunity to bring the project to fruition. In addition, there have been a number of individuals along the way whose kindness and confidence in me was a significant source of encouragement, especially Glen Schmidt at the University of Northern British Columbia, and Martha Wiebe and Hugh Armstrong from Carleton University's School of Social Work. Finally, I would be remiss if I did not thank the invaluable assistance of the University of Alberta Press, especially Mary Mahoney-Robson who shepherded the manuscript through review and revision stages, and stayed confident in me throughout, and Alethea Adair, who made it readable with her editorial skills.

AADAC – Alberta Alcohol and Drug Abuse Commission   xiii
ACHB – Alberta Child Health Benefit
AISH – Assured Income for the Severely Handicapped
CAFB – Canadian Association of Food Banks
CAP – Canada Assistance Plan
CCTB – Canada Child Tax Benefit
CHST – Canada Health and Social Transfer
CPI – Community Partnership Initiatives
CPP – Canada Pension Plan
CRISP – Child Related Income Support Program
EAPD – Employability Assistance for People with Disabilities
ECD – Early Childhood Development Agreement
EI – Employment Insurance
EIA – Employment and Income Assistance Program
ESIA – Employment Support and Income Assistance Program
NOFA – Family Assistance Act
FAS – Fetal Alcohol Syndrome
FAP – Financial Assistance Program (Prince Edward Island)
FESP – Federal Expenditures on Social Policy
EPF – Established Programs Financing Act
F/P/T – Federal/Provincial/Territorial
GAI – Guaranteed Annual Income
GIS – Guaranteed Income Supplement
GNP – Gross National Product
HALS – Health and Activity Limitation Survey
HASI – Home Adaptations for Senior's Independence
HRDC – Human Resources Development Canada
IAP – Income Assistance Program
ILBC – Independent Living British Columbia
ISBS – Income Support Benefit Services
LICO – Low Income Cut-Off

LIM – Low Income Measures
BM – Market Basket Measure
MHR – Ministry of Human Resources
MSP – Medical Services Plan
NAFTA – North American Free Trade Agreement
NCA – National Children's Agenda
NCB – National Child Benefit
NFLD/LAB – Newfoundland/Labrador
NLCB – Newfoundland and Labrador Child Benefit
NLHC – Newfoundland and Labrador Housing Corporation
NLSCY – National Longitudinal Survey of Children and Youth
N.S. – Nova Scotia
OAS – Old Age Security
OECD – Organization of Economic Cooperation and Development
P.E.I. – Prince Edward Island
PHRP – Provincial Housing Repair Program
PHI – Provincial Homelessness Initiative
PTA – Provincial Training Allowance
PWA – Parental Wage Assistance
RRAP – Residential Rehabilitation Assistance
SAFER – Shelter Aid for Elderly Renters
SAIL – Saskatchewan Aids to Independent Living
SCAP – Senior Citizens Assistance Program
SES – Saskatchewan Employment Supplement
SHC – Saskatchewan Housing Corporation
STD – Sexually Transmitted Diseases
SUFA – Social Union Framework Agreement
UI – Unemployment Insurance
UNICEF – United Nations International Children's Emergency Fund
VRDP – Vocational Rehabilitation for Disabled Persons
VSI – Voluntary Sector Initiative
VSSG – Voluntary Sector Steering Group

xiv

1

The Problem of Child Poverty in Canada

The increasing scope of child poverty in Canada has been high on the national agenda since at least 1989 when Ed Broadbent, leader of the New Democratic Party, proposed a resolution in the House of Commons to eliminate child poverty by 2000. The resolution passed unanimously and sparked the formation of Campaign 2000, a broad national coalition of non-governmental agencies committed to monitoring the government's progress toward that goal. More than a decade later, the September 2001 issue of *MacLean's*, a Canadian national news magazine, featured child poverty as its cover story: "Here we are in 2001...and child poverty in Canada is worse, not better."[1] This discourse on child poverty raises a number of issues around the scope and nature of child poverty in Canada. This chapter places these issues in epistemological context to examine the relationship between the social problem of child poverty and federal social policy.

Scope of Child Poverty in Canada: Facts and Perspectives

Facts are not neutral bits of information about objective reality but value-laden selections of information that reflect or suggest a perspective on reality that is itself selective. Consider, for example, the factual description of a glass of water as half empty or half full. Both descriptions of the glass's content can be simultaneously empirically valid, but the choice of which fact to present alters the perception of the context of the glass. This example is often used to demonstrate the difference between a pessimist and an optimist. Similarly, facts about child poverty are not value neutral. The 1989 House of Commons resolution marked a change in the framing of poverty discourse[2] in Canada from an issue of income distribution to one of aid for hapless victims of circumstances beyond their control. In this new context, facts about child poverty represented an issue of compassion, not of equity.

CHART 1–1: Child Poverty In Canada, 1980–2001

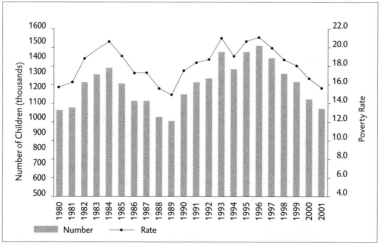

Source: Campaign 2000. *Honouring Our Promises: Meeting the Challenge to End Child and Family Poverty,* 2003. (pdf file accessible through http://campaign2000.ca/rc/rc03/index.html). 2003.

In a seminal study of this discourse, Wanda Wiegers argues that

> the dominance of a child poverty focus in state discourse reflects a restructuring process undertaken by governments over the last two decades. A focus on child poverty is consistent with a new policy emphasis on market outcomes and individual responsibility, a policy orientation toward targeting benefits and a pronounced concern with "work" incentives.[3]

While state discourse represents only one dimension of a broader public dialogue on an issue like child poverty, the discourse that ensued from the 1989 resolution gave an ideological spin to the problem that shaped the terms in which it was addressed. The scope of child poverty, for example, became framed as a household-centred problem of deprived children, rather than as a systemic problem of income distribution, following framed state discourse on poverty since 1944. The notion of framing is used in the sense of a discursive border around the definition of a social problem that links discourse to policy. In this case, it provided an ideological link between an institutional model of social policy focused on entitlements to a residual model of social policy centred on aid to the deserving poor. This transition was consistent with the restructuring that was already well underway in Canadian social policy, as will be discussed in subsequent chapters, and in fact had direct international counterparts.

CHART 1–2: Average Provincial Welfare Incomes And Low Income Cut-offs, 1990–2001

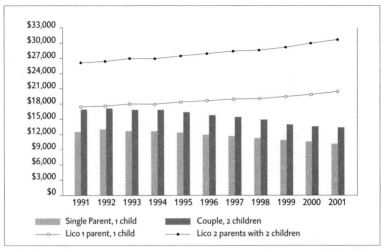

Source: Campaign 2000. *Poverty Amidst Prosperity, Campaign 2000 Report Card on Child and Family Poverty*, 2002. www.campaign2000.ca/rc/rc02/intro.html.

In the decade following the resolution, several coalitions of national, regional and local civil society organizations concerned with child and family issues were organized to promote public awareness of the plight of poor children.[4] They effectively championed the new framework in public discourse on poverty by advocating social policies targeted at poor children (as opposed to policies targeted at income redistribution). Campaign 2000, perhaps one of the best known because of its annual *Report Card on Child Poverty*, provides an archetypal example:

> Campaign 2000 is involved in public and government consultations around the issue of child and family poverty and government policy. We also lobby all parties in both federal and provincial governments for improved social policies relating to the national child benefit, social housing, child care, labour market supports, community services and other relevant policies.[5]

In its annual report cards, Campaign 2000 tracked the scope of child poverty. The 2003 report card established the government's failure "to honour" their commitment to eliminate child poverty.

The 2003 report noted that although "the numbers of children in poverty have declined in recent years, vulnerability and deep poverty in Canada have remained high."[6] The scope of child poverty, in other words, encompassed not only incidence but also the dimensions of vulnerability and depth. However, the dimension of vulnerability had been refocused from the basic needs perspective that had dominated public discourse on poverty in the post-World War II era to a perspective on household correlates, especially family type and labour market attachment. Similarly, the dimension of depth of poverty had been refocused from an assessment of the shortfall between income and basic needs satisfaction to a measure of the shortfall between the poverty line and household income. The confluence of these facts is reflected in Campaign 2000's report *Poverty Amidst Prosperity.*

This change in focus was reinforced by the research funding on child poverty made available by government agencies such as Human Resources Development Canada[7] to researchers, social policy institutes, and think tanks that promoted social policy research.[8] By the end of the decade, child poverty was generally accepted as a social problem—that is, as a social condition about which something should and could be done. The terms of reference essentially diagnosed the nature of "the problem" along the dimensions of vulnerability and depth, while intrinsically implying pathways of possible solutions. The National Council of Welfare's special report *Child Poverty Profile 1998* provided a summary of the terms of reference embedded in public discourse over the decade:

> The report examines child poverty by looking at children specifically and by looking at their families. Children are not poor on their own. They are poor because their families are poor. We start by examining poverty from 1980 to 1998 for children and their families. This is followed by snapshots of poverty in 1998 for many indicators such as family type, number and age of children in a family and age, education and work activity of parents.... Data is presented on the depth of poverty of children's families using indicators such as average dollars below the poverty line and family incomes as a percentage of the poverty line. There is a section on the sources of income of poor children's families. And finally, information is presented on the duration of poverty.[9]

Ideological Perspectives

As a link between discourse and policy, ideology can be understood as a system of beliefs and values about human nature and the nature of society that shape a sociopolitical worldview and legitimate a course of action.[10] Three ideological perspectives have been identified that have dominated the link between social problems discourse and social policy in Canada's

TABLE 1–1: Ideological Perspectives[12]

	Liberal Individualism	Ethical Liberalism	Social Democratic Liberalism
Nature of Society	*Core Belief*: a self-regulating system of interdependent parts; the market is a subsystem that provides the natural regulatory function	*Core Belief*: a non-self regulating system of interdependent parts. The market only provides a regulatory function if competition is fair	*Core Belief*: society is composed of interdependent groups organized around patterns of cooperation, competition, and conflict
	Core Value: non-interference in the natural functioning of the system; that is, the market provides the essential regulatory function through competition	*Core Value*: fair competition, humanitarianism, pragmatism, community spirit	*Core Value*: cooperation
	Policy Orientation: deregulation and privatization	*Policy Orientation*: regulation to ensure equality of opportunity (fair competition) and humanitarian provision to the poor, marginalized and dispossessed through community agencies	*Policy Orientation*: government provision of basic needs outside of market
Human Nature	*Core Belief*: egotistical, egocentric, and acquisitive	*Core Belief*: egotistical, egocentric, and acquisitive	*Core Belief*: human nature is multidimensional and adaptable and shaped by the dominant patterns of society
	Core Value: individualism, accumulation, competition, and inequality	*Core Value*: individualism, accumulation, competition, and inequality	*Core Value*: cooperation, altruism, and creativity
	Policy Orientation: protection of individual rights and property	*Policy Orientation*: emphasis on equality of opportunity for individuals	*Policy Orientation*: emphasis on equality of condition for individuals
Nature of Child Poverty[13]	*Core Belief*: innocent victims of parental Improvidence and/or ineptness	*Core Belief*: an individual or community problem	*Core Belief*: a byproduct of the market-driven economy promoted by liberal individualism
	Core Value: paternalistic to children; punitive to parents labeled undeserving	*Core Value*: paternalism; humanitarianism	*Core Value*: egalitarianism
	Policy Orientation: target benefits to children, with service delivery through market (proprietary and non-proprietary channels)	*Policy Orientation*: improve access to child welfare services	*Policy Orientation*: proactive intervention to ameliorate inequality

political culture.[11] They provide a means of conceptualizing the relationship between social problems' discourse and policy interventions on a social problem like child poverty.

The ideological perspectives that have been influential in Canadian social policy offer insight into the nature of the "ideological spin" on child poverty in state discourse. They also provide an ideological context for examining the transition from institutional to residual social policy models addressed in subsequent chapters.

The Problem in International Perspective

The problem of child poverty in Canada can also be examined from an international perspective. The 1989 House of Commons resolution, in fact, had an international counterpart in the 1989 United Nations "Convention on the Rights of the Child." In 1990 Canada's neo-liberal prime minister, Brian Mulroney, co-chaired the "World Summit for Children," in effect signaling that the same kind of ideological spin on child poverty developing at the national level would be also delivered at the international level.

The UNICEF Innocenti Research Centre,[14] established in 1988 to foster research "on the changing needs of children in both developing and industrialized countries," provided an important venue for developing and disseminating a comparative approach to child poverty as a problem of economic development.[15] Following the "World Summit for Children," the Centre initiated the report card series that "measures and compares the situation of children in OECD [Organization of Economic Cooperation and Development] countries." [16] With the publication of its first report card in June 2000—A League Table of Child Poverty in Rich Nations—the Centre announced: "This first Innocenti Report Card is intended as a contribution to the debate on how such poverty can best be defined, measured, and reduced."[17] Framing equality of opportunity as the nature of the problem of child poverty in rich nations, the report emphasized that

> ...the fact remains that the children of the poor simply do not have the same opportunities as the children of the non-poor. Whether measured by physical and mental development, health and survival rates, educational achievement or job prospects, incomes or life expectancies, those who spend their childhood in poverty of income and expectation are at a marked and measurable disadvantage.[18]

The problem for the children of the poor, in other words, is not poverty but competitive disadvantage. The policy implications of such a definition of the problem were dramatized in the Centre's report on child deaths by injury in rich countries. "The likelihood of a child being injured or killed appears to be strongly associated with such factors as poverty, single parenthood, low maternal education, low maternal age at birth, poor housing, large family size, and parental drug or alcohol abuse."[19] Identified as one of a number of discrete and disparate social problems—rather than the lifestyle correlates of poverty—in effect the relationship between poverty and risk of injury is diluted. Therefore, "the attempt to analyse and prevent child injury" is targeted at symptoms of poverty, not poverty.[20]

The UNICEF Innocenti Research Centre reflects an international discourse promoting an ideological spin on the serious and increasingly severe global social problem of poverty, disseminated largely through the organs and agencies of the United Nations, the World Bank, and the International Monetary Fund. The framing of child poverty as a problem of economic development in poor nations is consistent with the goals of economic development and globalization these agencies sponsor. Framing child poverty as a problem of competitive disadvantage in rich nations, on the other hand, serves to promote policy solutions consistent with the neo-liberal market economics of advanced capitalism. In this context, the Innocenti Centre's report card series was targeted at influencing public discourse, particularly civil society, among members of the European Union and the OECD.

A parallel discourse that emanated from the OECD was explicitly targeted at the high-ranking civil servants and policy makers of member governments for the expressed purpose of "helping governments tackle the economic, social and governance challenges of a globalized economy."[21] In contrast to the child poverty discourse advanced by the UNICEF Innocenti Research Centre, the poverty discourse that issued from the OECD was framed as an issue of economic competitiveness. The ideological spin driving the econometric and authoritative OECD discourse on poverty was set in 1996 at a "High-level Conference" of OECD members organized to set the social policy agenda for the twenty-first century:

> The slowdown in the growth of OECD economies over the past twenty-five years has been accompanied by fears about the sustainability of current systems of social protection. These concerns are increasingly focused on the growth in cash transfers: transfers to the elderly have increased, as have those to people not in employment, including not only unemployment benefits, but also (and increasingly) social assistance, invalidity and early retirement benefits. The relative gap between households at the top and bottom of the income distribution has widened in many countries. Maintaining lone parents and the long-term unemployed on benefits is seen as a problem rather than a solution.[22]

The discourse that proceeded from this perspective focused on examining the nature of the relationship between the household correlates and work attachment of the poor. In this context, children were identified as one of the correlates of poor households. For example, a study by Jean-Marc Burniaux, Thai-Thanh Dang, Douglas Fore, Michael Forster, Marco Mira d'Ercole and Howard Oxley on changes in income distribution and poverty in thirteen OECD countries, including Canada, concluded, "in general, individual households with no workers, in households with a young or an older head, and in households with children had below average income." The study suggested that "there may be scope for better targeting of [social] expenditures" but cautioned that "programmes need to be carefully designed and active measures that encourage employment should be favoured over passive measures that may discourage it."[23] As this reflects, the framing of poverty as a problem of economic competitiveness signals an orientation to policy that is consistent with that of child poverty discourse. However, OECD discourse frames the problem of poverty in terms of facts about the dynamics of the labour market–human capital nexus.

While the rational problem-solving approach to a systemic problem that pervades OECD discourse is in contrast to the moral crusade approach underpinning child poverty discourse, the policy prescriptions of the two discourses are markedly similar. Facts about poverty spun from the OECD perspective relate to identification and quantification of the relationship between low-income households and labour force participation common across rich countries.[24] From this context, the criteria for evaluation of policies and programs are explicit and rationalistic. In contrast, facts about poverty spun from the perspective of child poverty discourse focus on incidence and its correlates, and the criteria for evaluation are implicit and essentially moralistic.

Nature of Child Poverty in Canada: Measurement and Meaning

The first *Innocenti Report Card* compared child poverty rates across 23 rich countries on both relative and absolute measures. As the table reveals, on a measure of relative poverty (defined as households with income below 50 percent of the national median), Canada's child poverty rate was greater than 16 of 23 countries. In contrast, on a measure of absolute poverty (defined as households with incomes inadequate to purchase a fixed minimum of basic needs), Canada's child poverty rate was less than 12 of the 19 countries.

Facts are even more complex than the initial analogy of the glass of water suggested. Is the glass 70 percent empty or 63 percent full? Facts are artifacts of measurement that represent what is and is not measured

TABLE 1–2: Canada in International Perspective: Relative and Absolute Poverty

Relative Poverty		Absolute Poverty	
Country	Percent	Country	Percent
Sweden	2.6	Luxembourg	1.2
Norway	3.9	Norway	3.0
Finland	4.3	Denmark	5.1
Belgium	4.4	Sweden	5.3
Luxembourg	4.5	Finland	6.9
Denmark	5.1	Belgium	7.5
Czech Republic	5.9	**Canada**	**9.5**
Netherlands	7.7	France	10.7
France	7.9	Netherlands	11.1
Hungary	10.3	Germany	12.5
Germany	10.7	USA	13.9
Japan	12.2	Australia	16.2
Spain	12.3	Ireland	21.4
Greece	12.3	UK	29.1
Australia	12.6	Italy	36.1
Poland	15.4	Spain	42.8
Canada	**15.5**	Czech Republic	83.1
Ireland	16.8	Hungary	90.6
Turkey	19.7	Poland	93.1
UK	19.8		
Italy	20.5		
USA	22.4		
Mexico	26.2		

Source: A League Table of Child Poverty in Rich Nations, 4 7.

as a function of this process. For example, facts about an object such as a picture bring selected properties or characteristics of the object into relief and obscure others. In the context of a discourse, facts are artifacts of the measurement of what is represented as significant in a discursive frame. From this perspective, the measurement of child poverty not only conveys selected facts about child poverty but also conveys beliefs about the nature of poverty.

Consider, for example, the standard instrument for the measurement of child poverty in Canada, LICO. Like most members of the OECD (except the United States and the United Kingdom), Canada does not have an official poverty measure. Studies of poverty in rich nations, such as those produced by the OECD, rely on household income data to measure poverty. In the

TABLE 1–3: LICO and LIM Cut-offs for a Family of Four, 1995

Income	LICO*	LIM
Before-tax	$21,944–$31,753	$25,064
After-tax	$17,561–$26,785	$21,074

*Range based on community size—from rural to urban
Source: Income data from Bernard Paquet, *Low Income Cutoffs from 1992 to 2001 and Low Income Measures from 1991 to 2000.*

late 1960s Statistics Canada devised LICO (low-income cut-off rates that vary by size of family and community) and has produced them annually since 1971.[25] As an instrument for the measurement of child poverty, LICOs have generally been used to calculate child poverty in terms of the number of children in any given year living in households with incomes below LICO. Although not an official poverty rate, it is the most widely accepted measure of poverty in Canada. Households with incomes below the LICO rate are identified as low income—Statistics Canada's euphemism for poverty.[26] However, the LICO measure of poverty actually significantly under represents Canada's poverty rate as it does not include certain categories of people—including those living in the territories, in institutions, on Native reservations, and members of the armed forces. Originally devised to assess low income in an era when poverty was framed as an issue of income distribution in public discourse in Canada and Europe, by 1989 LICO had essentially become institutionalized as the standard for measuring poverty in Canada and provided a standardized time-series database for assessing the incidence of child poverty.

Changes in Statistics Canada's calculation of the LICOs are indicative of the changing ideological spin on poverty in state discourse. Reflecting the ideological spin of the era,[27] LICO was formulated as an explicitly relative measure of the "income threshold below which a family will likely devote a larger share of its income to the necessities of food, shelter and clothing than an average family would."[28] The estimation of average family expenditures was based on periodic *Family Expenditure Surveys* (1959, 1969, 1978, 1986, and 1992), updated annually in-between base years to adjust for inflation using the consumer price index. LICOs varied by the base year of the *Family Expenditure Survey* used in their calculation. As a measure of low income or poverty, in other words, the number of poor depended on the LICO base year used. Based on a snap-shot portrait of community standards as reflected in both average income and average expenditures on necessities at a given time, LICO provided a static measure of the standard of living below the prevailing norm in a community. For comparability across time, the same LICO base year has to be utilized. Standardized data on low

TABLE 1–4: The Gap Filled by the Market Basket Measure

Concept of Poverty	Method of Measurement	
	Absolute	Relative
Subsistence	Sarlo	
Creditability (i.e., deserving)	Market Basket Measure	After-tax LIM
Social Inclusion	Community Social Planning Council of Toronto	LICOs and LIMs

income are provided by Statistics Canada. However, the dynamic of change in community standards is essentially lost.

Prior to 1978, published LICO rates were based on a household's pre-tax total income, including government transfers. Beginning in 1980 after-tax LICOs were also calculated, but as they were derived independently from pre-tax LICOs and had "no simple relationship" with them, they were not readily available. They reflected a lower poverty rate as the number of people falling below the cut-offs was lower on an after-tax basis than on a before-tax basis.[29] Nevertheless, the pre-tax LICO remained the standard poverty measure throughout the decade. After major user consultations, in 1991 Statistics Canada initiated publication of LIMs (Low Income Measures). Low income cut-off rates based on 50 percent of median income adjusted for family size and composition on the basis of an equivalence scale instead of the *Family Expenditure Survey* used in LICOs, but did not adjust for community size as LICO provided.[30] As with LICOs, both before- and after-tax LIMs were published. The difference between the two measures in the low income cut-offs is reflected in Table 1–3.

On LIM, the poverty rate for the total population was lower on the before-tax measure than it was on the after-tax LICO. When disaggregated by age, the poverty rate for seniors registered an even sharper decline than the LICO. However, it registered a higher poverty rate for children.[31] Thus, LIM was effectively discredited by its failure to register a lower child poverty rate and attention refocused on LICO.[32] Throughout the 1990s, the after-tax LICO was the standard measure of poverty in state discourse but was not widely used in public discourse.[33] To highlight the after-tax LICOs and make them more readily available to the public, from 1998 the two sets of LICO rates (before and after taxes) were available simultaneously, and as of 2001 all low income cut-offs were published in the same publication.[34]

Nevertheless, the income inequality philosophy and standard-of-living methodology underlying LICO rendered it a fundamentally incongruent measure of poverty in a discourse framed in terms of aid, not entitlements. "Virtually every release of low income results," noted the Statistics Canada working paper, "triggers public discussion on the LICO measure itself. In

TABLE 1–5: Child Poverty by LICO: 1978, 1986 and 1992 Base Years

	Campaign 2000 (000)	1978 base before tax (000)	1986 base before tax (000)	1986 base after tax (000)	1992 base before tax (000)	1992 base after tax (000)
1971		2,574				
1972		2,236				
1973		2,057				
1974		1,634				
1975		1,313				
1976		1,217				
1977		1,186				
1978		1,045				
1979		1,044				
1980		968			1,066	815
1981		1,073			1,085	827
1982		1,236			1,248	928
1983		1,260			1,294	1,020
1984		1,325			1,345	1,029
1985		1,240			1,243	1,006
1986		1,120	1,108	917	1,149	897
1987		1,035	1,088	931	1,151	909
1988		945	1,017	836	1,054	819
1989	936	907	980	815	1,016	786
1990	1,106	1,060	1,136	931	1,195	893
1991	1,212	1,207	1,223	1,012	1,282	986
1992	1,279	1,234	1,245	1,023	1,317	988
1993	1,455	1,383			1,455	1,083
1994	1,331	1,304			1,331	1,024
1995	1,447	1,389			1,447	1,138
1996	1,484	1419			1,448	1,175
1997	1,405	1309	1,393	1,176	1,416	1,131
1998	1,307	1138	1,303	1,059	1,338	978
1999	1,251				1,251	940
2000	1,139				1,139	868
2001					1,071	786

particular, there is concern that the LICO is 'too high'."[35] However, the problem was deeper than that. Neo-liberal think tanks like the Fraser Institute initiated an attack on the concept of relative poverty with the publication of Christopher Sarlo's treatise *Poverty in Canada* in 1992.[36]

Human Resources Development Canada (HRDC) took the initiative in developing a measure of poverty more consistent with the deserving/undeserving poor philosophy of neo-liberal poverty discourse and established a Federal/Provincial/Territorial (F/P/T) Working Group on Social Development Research and Information. In 1998, it announced preliminary development of a Market Basket Measure (MBM). "The Market Basket Measure is based on the concept of 'necessities' which was defined by Adam Smith as 'whatever the custom of the country renders it indecent for creditable people, even of the lowest order, to be without.'"[37] While the poverty rate generated by the preliminary MBM was comparable to that generated by the after-tax LIM, the philosophy and methodology underlying it are not. Noting the debate over poverty measures in public discourse, HRDC's Applied Research Bulletin observed "differing concepts of poverty underlie the disagreement on poverty measures," and summarized the differences accordingly.[38] (See Table 1–4.)

Focused on consumption rather than expenditures, MBM is based on the cost of a basket of necessary goods and services to cover essentials, which is then used to define the level of disposable income needed to cover the cost of essentials. In addition, the concept of disposable income is less transparent and more restrictive than the after-tax income used in the low-income cut-off measures. For example, it excludes expenses such as support payments, work-related child-care costs and employee contributions to pension plans and Employment Insurance,[39] as well as benefits such as employer contributions to pension plans and extended health insurance, vacations, employment related relocation, and educational upgrading.

In spite of efforts to frame an alternative measure of poverty, however, LICO has remained the standard measure in the public sector. Table 1–5, "Child Poverty by LICO: 1978, 1986 and 1992 Base Years," reflects the impact of variations of the standard measure on assessment of the scope of child poverty, illustrating the confluence between meaning and measurement, and the significance of measurement consistency.

Impact of Child Poverty: Significance and Assessment

In the context of a discourse, facts signify the attribution of significance as well as meaning. The measurement of child poverty, in other words, not only conveys beliefs about the nature of poverty but also its significance. Indicative of the significance attributed to the problem at the time, following the 1989 House of Commons resolution, the Standing Senate Committee on Social Affairs, Science and Technology was authorized to "examine and report upon the relationship between childhood poverty and certain significant and costly social problems. . .."[40] Its final report, generally referred to as the Marsden report, submitted in January 1991, identified impact in terms of the unfair disadvantage that confronted poor children, citing evidence on two significant dimensions: health and education. "To be born poor is to have the deck stacked against you at birth, to find life an uphill struggle ever after. To be born poor is unfair to kids."[41]

From the perspective of the Senate Committee, the significance of child poverty related to the assessment of equality of opportunity as the basis of a just society—an ideological cornerstone of the welfare state. However, the ideological context of welfare state discourse on social problems reflected in the Marsden report was already passé in Ottawa by 1989; there was virtually no further state discourse on child poverty. In its place, a discourse on child development began to take shape, and in 1992 the National Longitudinal Survey of Children and Youth (NLSCY) was initiated to produce a new database of facts on child development. The NLSCY was instituted as a joint project of HRDC and Statistics Canada to provide a single source of data for the examination of child development in context by developing a national database on the characteristics and life experiences of Canadian children.[42] The project was designed to track an initial sample of 15,000 children, aged 0–11, until age 25. Seven cycles of data collection were planned, beginning with cycle 1 in 1994 and culminating in cycle 7 in 2006, with a cohort of newborns added to each cycle. The new database's purpose "of bringing children's issues to the forefront" and stimulating the emergence of a public discourse on child development was advanced with the development of a research program.[43] By 1998, the project's newsletter, *Developments,* announced "a substantial number of HRDC-funded research projects are now underway. . .analyzing the cycle 1 data."[44]

The child development frame was also being extended beyond state discourse and into civil society. In 1997 the Speech from the Throne announced that "the federal, provincial and territorial governments agreed in January 1997 to work together to develop the National Children's Agenda (NCA), a comprehensive strategy to improve the well-being of Canada's children. . .," and that the federal government would "establish Centres of Excellence to deepen our understanding of children's development and well-being. . .."[45] In 2000 the Government of Canada committed $20 million over five years for the creation of five centres of excellence for children's well-being to "bring together front line health care practitioners with academics and researchers to address issues of national significance affecting the health and well-being of Canadian children."[46]

In the child development frame, the problem of child poverty essentially dissipated into a plethora of problems related to child development, and the social problem of child poverty, so high on the public agenda in the 1990s, dissolved into the problem of child vulnerability. To define the terms of reference of child vulnerability under the child development frame and propagate the facts "among scholars who are dedicated to conducting policy relevant research," the HDRC sponsored a

> training program...to teach scholars who were early in their careers some of the more advanced statistical methods applicable to analyzing data from the...NLSCY. These scholars worked closely with members of the NLSCY Expert Advisory Committee to bring together a set of papers about the factors that affect children's development.[47]

A volume of research articles entitled *Vulnerable Children* resulted from the program. Utilizing data from cycle 1 of the NLSCY, in effect the volume set the terms of reference of the problem of vulnerability in terms of its nature and scope. The lead article defined vulnerability in terms of "children who are experiencing an episode of poor developmental outcomes."[48] Indicative of the distinctly ideological spin of neo-liberalism, developmental outcomes are measured in terms of a child's development of cognitive, motor and social skills—a skill set directly related to competitive individualism. In the changed ideological context of state discourse, the image of the competitive society had replaced the just society in the assessment of impact. Furthermore, the crude stereotypes of child poverty underpinning the moralistic appeal of child poverty discourse were essentially statistically pacified in the assessment of child development:

> The relationship between children's outcomes and family income is so firmly entrenched in our understanding of human development that the term "children at risk" has almost become synonymous with "children living in poverty." It is easy to presume that the majority of children with behaviour problems or poor academic results are from low-income families; or conversely, that children with model behaviour and strong academic skills are predominantly from affluent families. ...Although there may be a gradient associated with family income, we often encounter children from poor families who have been remarkably more resilient, and children from affluent families who have behavioural or academic difficulties.[49]

In the terms of reference of the NLSCY, poverty may be a matter of fact in the sense of socio-economic stratification, but it is not a significant problem. The marginalization of poverty discourse that this reflects is not unique to Canada. It is an international phenomenon that is the outcome

15

of a global process of ideological change initiated with the collapse of the Soviet Union and end of the cold war.[50]

Federal Social Policy and Child Poverty

The existence of a federal discourse on child poverty is itself anomalous in terms of Canada's constitution. As a federation, Canada has two levels of government—federal and provincial—and each level is assigned specific powers in the constitution. The constitution gives the provinces jurisdiction over the administration of justice, municipal institutions, and the establishment and maintenance of prisons, hospitals, asylums, and charitable institutions. The federal government has jurisdiction over defense, criminal law, regulation of trade and commerce, banking, currency, rates and measures, inter-provincial transportation and communication, and other matters primarily related to economic development.[51] As a result of the constitutional mandate, then, social policy matters are under provincial jurisdiction, and the problem of child poverty is outside federal jurisdiction. This raises a moot question at the outset: why is the federal government involved in a discourse on child poverty and social policy?

The issue of poverty has been a catalyst for policy change in Canada at least since the Great Depression, and in the aftermath of World War II, it was a central concern in post-war planning. Three major rounds of state discourse on poverty punctuated the twentieth century, each culminating in a major federal social policy initiative—the post-depression round that culminated in the Marsh report in 1943 and the development of the Canadian welfare state over the next thirty years; Canada's "war on poverty" round initiated in the mid 1960s that culminated in the *Social Security Review* of 1973; and the child poverty round initiated in 1989 with the House of Commons resolution on child poverty.

While each of these initiatives and the changes in federal social policy they entailed are discussed in some detail in subsequent chapters, it should be noted at the outset that the anomaly of federal social policy has been a contentious political issue in the framework of Canadian federalism. The emergence of a significant federal role in social policy was catalyzed by the scope and magnitude of impoverishment and dispossession brought on by the Great Depression. The constitutional compartmentalization of social policy broke down in the efforts to meet the policy challenges posed. Without encompassing constitutional change, in the post World War II era the federal government became a central architect of social policy in Canada by virtue of its spending power, which it used to construct the principles, plans and course of action for provincial social policy development throughout the remainder of the century. State discourse on poverty in each round served as a forerunner to shifts in the principles legitimating federal action in the social policy sphere. Federal government shifts, marked by changing patterns of federal expenditures on social policy, manifest changes in its course of action in the social policy sphere. The following chapters examine federal social policy in terms of policy principles, plans, and course of action over the second half of the twentieth century.

2

The Canadian Welfare State and the Growth of Entitlement

The development of the Canadian welfare state encompassed the post-Depression and World War II on poverty rounds of state discourse. It entailed fundamental change in the political economy of Canadian social policy in both the nature and scope of welfare benefits and in the processes by which they were determined. This chapter examines both dimensions to recount the story of the Canadian welfare state.

Nature and Scope of Welfare Benefits

Welfare benefits can be defined generally as in-cash or in-kind services distributed outside the market system. As the market is the central vehicle in capitalist society for the distribution of goods and services, the nature of welfare benefits is fundamentally linked to their relationship with the market. The market is legitimated in liberal theory as the venue for the satisfaction of human wants. Post-Depression poverty discourse maintained it was an inappropriate medium for the satisfaction of human needs. After all, exchange in the market directed by a profit motive and profit making—on the backs of the needy, if not at their expense—has been considered reprehensible in most social traditions.[1] Richard Titmus (1976), an eminent British scholar on social policy, made the case against market transfer, arguing that social needs are "predominantly dependent needs, which the market does not or cannot satisfy for certain designated sections of the population."[2]

The epistemological distinction between needs and wants, then, was critical to the welfare state concept. C.B. Macpherson[3] identified four discernibly different positions in political theory related to the issue of needs and wants: Rousseau; liberal individualism; ethical liberalism; and Marx. Because the distinctions between needs and wants have been at the very core of ideological debate about the welfare state, it is important to overview each of these schools.

Rousseau

Jean-Jacques Rousseau (1712–78), a Swiss-French philosopher, treated wants and needs in both a historical and an ontological manner. The central question of Rousseau's thought was: how do individuals reconcile to the demands of society? Rousseau attempted to make distinctions between "natural" and "artificial" *besoins* (needs/wants). Needs he described in terms of physical drives—food, sex, and repose; wants were anything else. With the rise of civil society (and all its inequality and oppression), many wants evolved into needs through habit. The intense competitive desire to acquire and accumulate in capitalist civil society encouraged man to have infinite wants that they qualified as need; these are artificial needs. An insidious evolution occurs where "the artificial needs displace the natural ones in importance as determinants of men's behavior."[4]

Liberal Individualism

This term is used to describe the form of individualism that ranges from the classical political economists and the utilitarians (Hume 1711–76, Adam Smith 1723–90, Bentham 1748–1832) to most of the twentieth-century economic theorists. The essential postulate of this liberal individualism is that every individual's wants naturally increase without limit. The beliefs of liberal individualism are founded on the premise that the need for endless wants is good (this is the antithesis of Rousseau). A closer examination of this theory illustrates that there is no separation between needs (natural) and wants (artificial). In contrast, it is assumed that if you want it, you must need it. Modern liberal individualists have taken this one step further to suggest that the root distinction among wants and needs may be culturally determined.

Ethical Liberalism

This term encompasses the liberal philosophies of John Stuart Mill (1806–73), and his twentieth-century successors in both the neo-idealist and modified utilitarian traditions. The distinction between ethical liberalism and classical liberalism is that the former rejected the supposition that all wants were equally good. Ethical liberalists believed that the "quality of want-satisfaction and therefore of wants, was as important as the quantity."[5] Ethical liberalism conceptually is inadequate as an explanation for needs and wants

> because, although it sees the possibility (and desirability) of wants changing for the better in the future, it pays little attention to how they have developed up to the present. It does not see that the present want-

schedules, which it deplores, are the product and inevitable concomitant of the capitalist market society, which it accepts.[6]

Marx

Karl Marx (1818–83) clearly rejected Rousseau's notions of natural/artificial. Marx contended that Benthamists and classical economists provided

> an accurate portrayal of what human wants are reduced to in capitalist society (or any society based on private property), that is, the wants of alienated man. In alienated society all the senses have been reduced to the sense of having, of possessing. Thus, wants are reduced to what gratifies the sense of having.[7]

21

Marx held that the truly human need was unalientated labour. Beyond this, Macpherson maintains that Marx was ambiguous on the nature of needs. However, others suggest that he did make a distinction between true and false needs.[8] On this formulation, Patricia Springborg, an eminent political theorist, asserts:

> True to the Hegelian formula for dichotomies, false needs are those in which appearances substitute for reality. Needs which are false pose as their opposite, and thereby displace true needs: for example money, which pretends to mediate between man and his needs, but actually places their satisfaction further out of reach of those who sell their labour to have it. With Marx, for the first time, 'true' or 'false' needs are to be understood literally. This means that needs, like other features of the real world, are susceptible of truth and falsity and the distinction between reality and appearance. True needs are claimed to be objective in the sense that they represent real processes. ...[9]

The conception of needs imbedded in the epistemology of social welfare is grounded in ethical liberalism. Abraham Maslow's hierarchy of needs is the paramount formulation in the social welfare paradigm. Maslow identified a hierarchy of five categories of need, which he posited are instinctive and universal:

1. Physical needs—air, water, food, sex, etc.
2. Safety needs
3. Affection or belongingness needs
4. Esteem needs
5. Self-actualization needs

The first two categories in the hierarchy are essentially physiological, while the remaining levels progress from social to self-development needs. Any conception of welfare benefits generally subsumes the ontology of this hierarchy. However, the formulation has been critiqued as being meta-physical, ahistorical and mechanistic.[10] Nevertheless, contemporary needs theory has its roots in Maslov's formulation.[11]

As the cornerstone of capitalism, the market has been an issue of political debate especially present when examining the twentieth century's most significant capitalist crisis—the Great Depression. In their seminal work, Ideology and Social Welfare (1985), Vic George and Paul Wilding[12] identified orientation to market regulation as the central issue of theoretical debate within liberalism that emerged as a result of the challenge to capitalism posed by the Depression. They identified two schools of thought in this debate that directly equate with liberal individualism and ethical liberalism—which they labeled the anti-collectivists and collectivists. George and Wilding argued that for liberal individualists:

> the free market is the foundation of the self-generating and spontaneous order in social affairs which they regard with veneration. More specifically, they see the market system as a vital bulwark of political freedom, as the most efficient system of economic relations yet devised and as the great engine of economic growth. Its success depends only on being left alone by governments once a basic legal and monetary framework has been provided.[13]

While ethical liberalism accepts the veracity and superiority of capitalism, the Depression seriously undermined the proposition that the market is self-regulating. Ethical liberalists maintain that the unregulated competition of the free market is wasteful and inefficient:

> It fails to use the productive capacity of the economy to the full and it grossly misallocates resources. Of itself, it will not operate so as to abolish injustice and poverty. Furthermore, rather than being a vital foundation for a self-generating and spontaneous political order, it will create conditions directly threatening to political stability if left to operate without government oversight.[14]

In summary, beliefs about the nature of welfare benefits derive from beliefs about the market on the one hand, and needs/wants on the other. Given the ideological character of both of these concepts, it is not surprising that the issue of welfare benefits was at the centre of political debate in the ideological transition to liberal individualism that marked the last

TABLE 2–1: Ideological Perspectives on Welfare Benefits

	Liberal Individualism	Ethical Liberalism	Social Democratic Liberalism
Nature of Welfare Benefits	*Core belief:* social philanthropy based on individual subscription	*Core belief:* social philanthropy based on voluntary donation	*Core belief:* guaranteed access to basic needs a right of citizenship
	Core value: volunteerism	*Core value:* humanitarianism	*Core value:* egalitarianism
	Policy orientation: promotion of social philanthropy with tax incentives	*Policy orientation:* provision for the basic needs of the deserving poor through community agencies	*Policy orientation:* public provision of basic needs outside the market
Scope of Public Welfare Benefits	*Core belief:* public provision undermines self-reliance and encourages dependency	*Core belief:* an institutional infrastructure of public welfare benefits is necessary to level the playing field of capitalism for the disadvantaged	*Core belief:* an institutional infrastructure of public welfare benefits is necessary to ameliorate the social injustices of capitalism
	Core value: paternalism	*Core value:* equality of opportunity	*Core value:* poverty reduction
	Policy orientation: only as a last resort and targeted at the deserving poor	*Policy orientation:* public provision to ameliorate socio-economic disadvantages	*Policy orientation:* public provision to support a basic standard of living for all citizens

quarter of the twentieth century. From an ideological perspective, the scope of welfare benefits derives from beliefs about its nature.

The scope of welfare benefits may be described in terms of the type and range of social programs favoured by an ideological perspective. In the residual welfare model promoted by liberal individualism, the provision of welfare benefits is primarily a function of private philanthropy and civil society initiatives. Public welfare is an agency of last resort. As a result, localized voluntary programs that target selective categories of the deserving poor are promoted under liberal individualism. In the institutional achievement model advanced by ethical liberalism, civil society is a primary actor in the provision of selective, localized welfare programs for the deserving poor. The bulwark of social welfare, however, is based on an infrastructure of universal public welfare programs that provide basic benefits to categories of the population deemed systematically disadvantaged by the exigencies and contingencies of the capitalist economy. In contrast, social democratic liberalism fosters the advancement of an institutional redistributive model that guarantees a basic standard of living to all citizens, financed through a progressive tax structure.

Post-Depression Round

The concept of a welfare state refers to a state's commitment to ensure a minimum standard of living for its citizens. In the aftermath of the Great Depression, it was popularized and institutionalized in the capitalist states of Western Europe and North America in an effort to save capitalism from socialism. Richard Simeon, an eminent student of Canadian politics, identified three central characteristics of the post-Depression political climate that facilitated the emergence of the welfare state: a policy blueprint; political accommodation; and an accommodation of values.[15] The policy blueprint, which incorporated both economic and social dimensions, provided a framework for policy development. On the economic dimension, the blueprint was based on support for the Keynesian economic agenda. On the social dimension, the blueprint incorporated a commitment to the construction of a comprehensive safety net of social security programs and social infrastructure (health, education, etc.).[16] The Canadian welfare state was based on a political accommodation amongst the major social forces of the time—government, business, labour, and agriculture. The government's main role became one of assuring economic/market stability, providing a healthy competent working population, and instituting a social security system to ensure the costs for those outside the labour market. The goal of this accommodation was to guarantee that business/the market would flourish. "Workers would enjoy rising incomes, greater protection of health and safety, and relative security."[17] An *accommodation of values,* Simeon maintained, was based on:

> Bridging the gap between efficiency and equity, between economic growth and social justice.... Business was provided with a secure, educated work force and a stable economy, leaving it free to generate jobs and profits. This, in turn, generated the financial resources with which to finance the stronger social safety net. Growth and equity could go hand in hand, each reinforcing the other.[18]

F. Gustav Moller, one of the key architects of Sweden's model welfare state, identified three main principles as the cornerstones of the welfare state:[19]

- to guarantee a basic minimum standard of living for every citizen;
- to provide for social welfare as an inherent right for everyone regardless of income; and
- to meet these goals through the equalization of income and social justice.

However, "few students of comparative social policy," observed one comparative social policy analyst, "would seriously contend that the Canadian welfare state approximates Sweden's in terms of generosity, comprehensiveness or efficacy."[20] Rather, the Canadian welfare state was patterned on the British model. In 1942, Sir William Beveridge prepared a plan for British postwar reconstruction. The Beveridge report recommended a comprehensive social security program to protect income against interruptions due to social contingencies. It included children's allowances to protect against impoverishment due to family size, a universal health service, full employment, and a national housing program. In Canada's case, the cornerstone of the Canadian welfare state was laid by Leonard Marsh in his Report on Social Security in Canada, submitted to the Advisory Committee on Reconstruction in 1943. He proposed a comprehensive social security framework to protect workers' income against basic contingencies—unemployment, sickness and medical care, disability, old age and retirement, premature death, and family needs.[21] "The purpose of this report," Marsh maintained in the report's Prefatory Note,

> ...is an attempt to set out (a) the main features of existing statutory provisions for social security matters in Canada; (b) the methods by which these provisions can be improved and extended, particularly by transformation of the coverage and the technique to a social insurance basis; and (c) the principles which should be considered if the construction of a comprehensive social security system, suited to Canadian conditions, is to be undertaken in the most fruitful and effective manner.[22]

While not all his recommendations were adopted, the Marsh report "was a pivotal document in the development of war and postwar social security programs, the equivalent in Canada of the Beveridge Report in Great Britain."[23] It established the Canadian welfare state's basic principles of insurance and universality, but the rudimentary programs initially legislated in the post-Depression round covered only the most elementary risks to income while at the same time preserving the deserving/undeserving ethic of liberal individualism. Even before the Marsh report, the Depression had forced the federal government to venture into the housing market with the Dominion Housing Act of 1935. This marked the formal beginning of housing policy in Canada. The primary purpose of the Act was to shore up the housing market by introducing a joint mortgage-lending program to help finance housing construction and ownership. It was not until 1936 that a social policy dimension was added when the Dominion Housing Act was replaced with the National Housing Act. This National Housing Act not only extended the legislation of the 1935 Dominion Housing Act, it

25

also introduced assistance to low income families in attaining housing, and represented the first Canadian social housing legislation. It made provision for municipal development of low-rent housing. During World War II, the Crown's Wartime Housing Corporation built almost 46,000 units over an eight-year period, mostly for war workers, and helped repair and modernized thousands of existing units at a cost of $253 million. Accompanying this initiative was the expansion of the National Housing Act in 1944 to include federal-provincial programs to construct publicly owned and provincially managed housing for vulnerable groups—low-income families, seniors and the disabled.

Unlike federal legislation in the housing domain, it took a constitutional amendment to allow legislation of the Unemployment Insurance Act in 1940, "to protect the normal standard of living of the wage earner."[24] The new Act typified the ideological tension between liberal individualism and ethical liberalism. Benefits and contributions were wage related, with benefits to be provided as a right established by contributions. To be eligible for benefits, however, workers had to have been employed for at least 180 days over the two years preceding a claim, and demonstrate that they were capable and available for work. This compulsory program aimed at covering 75 percent of wage earners, but actually only ended up covering about 42 percent of the labour force.[25] Excluded from coverage were 21 categories of workers, including agricultural, "forestry, fishing, private domestic service, government and police forces, nurses and teachers, workers in hospitals and charitable institutions, and most classes of workers earning $2,000.00 or more."[26] Payments and benefits were to be actuarially related (except for low paid workers), with benefit levels at one half of the wage rate. The program was financed by contributions from the federal government, the employer and the employee, and was administered by the federal government.

The Family Allowance Act of 1944 was Canada's first universal social program. Financed out of general revenue and administered by the federal government,[27] it incorporated two expressed objectives: to serve the well-being of all Canadian children; and to buttress spending power in the post-World War II period. Benefits under the program were payable to all children (generally to their mothers) born in Canada under the age of sixteen or with three years residence prior to application. In 1949, the Act was amended to reduce the residency requirement to one year and to remove benefit reductions on the fifth and subsequent children in a family.[28]

Throughout the 1950s and 1960s, the federal government pursued the substance if not the letter of the Marsh report and actively promoted the development of a range of social security and social welfare programs. The Old Age Security Act was legislated in 1951 to replace the cost-shared and

TABLE 2–2: Policy Framework of the Canadian Welfare State, 1965

Programme	Federal Transfer Recipient	Policy
Income security:		
- Social insurance	- Unemployed	- Unemployment Insurance (1940; amended in 1955)
- Universal	- Families with Children	- Family Allowances (1944)
	- Elderly	- Old Age Security (1951)
Health insurance	- Provinces	- Health Insurance and Diagnostic Services Act (1957)
Higher education	- Institutions of higher education	- Higher Education Grants (1959)
Housing	- municipalities	- National Housing Act (1938, amended 1964)
	- war-workers	- Wartime Housing Corporation (Crown Corporation)
	- Provinces	- Expansion of the National Housing Act (1944); amended in 1964
Equalization	- Provinces	- Equalization grants (1957; 1962 formula revision)

means-tested Old Age Pension Act of 1927, and was financed by the federal government from general tax revenues. As a universal demogrant program, all Canadian citizens and legal residents 65 years and older were eligible to receive benefits upon application. In 1955 the Unemployment Insurance Act was amended and substantially overhauled. The most important changes were the inclusion of supplementary benefits, relaxation of entrance requirements, reduction of the maximum benefit duration, and increases in the maximum benefit period.

In 1957 an equalization program was introduced to reduce fiscal disparities among the provinces and enable less wealthy provinces to provide a level of public services comparable to wealthier provinces. The program provided unconditional grants to provinces based on a formula subject to periodic review. In 1957, the formula used the revenue-generating capacity of the two wealthiest provinces, British Columbia and Ontario, as the standard. In 1962, the payment formula was changed to an all-province average.

In 1964, the National Housing Act (NHA) was amended to allow commercial redevelopment of urban land purchased with federal funds under the NHA. The amendment linked the private profit motive with public funding and created a frenzy of garish urban renewal schemes that resulted in "the brutal clearance of low-income families from their cherished neighborhoods."[29]

The federal government's role in funding health and higher education was initiated on separate tracks under the welfare state framework of the post-World War II era. In the field of health, passage of the *Hospital Insurance and Diagnostic Services Act* in 1957 initiated public health insurance by providing for the federal government to cost-share with the provinces on a 50–50 basis, public health insurance plans for hospital services. The situation for higher education was different. The federal government instituted student grants to war veterans. After 1950, this program was superseded with grants directly to universities and colleges to facilitate their expansion in order to accommodate veterans. In 1959, these grants were replaced by an agreement with the provinces whereby the federal government made grants to higher education through the provinces.

Table 2–2 summarizes the policy framework of the Canadian welfare state in 1965, on the eve of initiation of the war on poverty round.

War on Poverty Round

The second round of state discourse on poverty in Canada was actually triggered by the much-hyped American "war on poverty," declared in 1964 by United States President Lyndon Johnson. In the foreword to the first Canadian book-length scholarly treatise on poverty, H. Edward Mann (1970) observed:

> For some years now the study of poverty has become an "in" thing, socially respectable and even of interest to governments. President Johnson gave this new trend—or fad—the official stamp of approval when he sponsored, in a blaze of publicity, the beginning of a War on poverty. Canada followed shortly afterwards. ...[30]

On April 5, 1965, the Liberal government's throne speech declared Canada's war on poverty with the announcement of two major social programs—the Canada Assistance Plan (CAP) and the Canada Pension Plan (CPP). CAP was initiated "to consolidate all the federal-provincial programs based on tests of means or needs into a single, comprehensive program of benefits that would meet financial need regardless of cause."[31] Legislated in 1966, CAP was a conditional grant program that provided for the federal government to contribute half of the cost of provincial assistance programs. In effect, the conditions reflected the objectives of the program: to base social assistance eligibility on needs, irrespective of cause; to eliminate means tests from provincial social assistance eligibility criteria; as well as to remove provincial residency requirements as a condition for provincial

28

social assistance. Thus, to be eligible for a federal grant under the Canada Assistance Plan, a provincial social assistance program had to meet these criteria. There was no upper limit on the federal contribution, and virtually no other constraints on provincial discretion. However, within one year of signing an agreement with the federal government, a province had to establish an administrative process for client appeals.

The Canada Assistance Plan had three parts: Part I provided for cost-sharing of general assistance and welfare services; Part II provided special provisions for cost-sharing welfare programs to "Indians registered under the Indian Act"; and Part III provided for the cost-sharing of work-activity projects for the hard-to-employ unemployed. All of the provinces except Quebec entered into agreements with the federal government under Part I of the plan to cost-share social assistance and welfare services. No agreements were ever made under Part II. All of the provinces funded work activity projects under Part III of the plan.[32] Considered "the best anti-poverty program achievable within the narrow confines of the traditional social assistance approach,"[33] CAP improved social assistance to the poor by improving benefits and access to benefits. In effect, it reduced the depth of poverty but not its incidence.

Also announced in 1965, the Canada Pension Plan was enacted to provide retirement, disability and survivor pensions, and a lump sum death benefit. The program's stated objectives were "to make reasonable minimum levels of income available on normal retirement ages, and to people who become disabled and to dependents of people who die."[34] The CPP is wage related and financed by combined contributions from the employer and the employee; it is compulsory and covers all employees between the ages of 18 years and 70 years. To provide protection of pension benefits against inflation, the legislation made benefits increase automatically in conjunction with increases in the cost of living, but only up to a maximum of two percent per year. Commenting on the significance of these increases, Guest notes that this program "marked the beginning of an attempt to replace... ad hoc measures [to adjust social security benefits to the cost of living] with some type of automatic, inflation-proof mechanism."[35]

In addition to the introduction of CAP and the CPP in 1965, the eligibility age for OAS was lowered from 70 to 65, and pension indexation was introduced. In 1966, the war on poverty was expanded into the health field with the introduction of the Medical Act, which expanded public health insurance to cover doctor visits. In 1967 two new programs were introduced: the Guaranteed Income Supplement (GIS), a selective needs-tested program to supplement the income of low-income elderly; and the Federal-Provincial Fiscal Arrangements Act, which based grants to the provinces for higher education on a system of tax transfers and cash grants to fund

29

post-secondary education. Changes to the equalization formula in 1967 were made to configure payments based on equalization to the national average. As a result of escalating provincial revenues in the early 1970s due to increasing resource revenues, under this standard almost all of the provinces were qualified to receive equalization payments.

Highlighting the persistence of public discourse on the problem of poverty, the fifth annual review of the Economic Council of Canada in 1968 noted:

> Poverty in Canada is real. Its numbers are not in the thousands, but the millions. There is more of it than our society can tolerate, more than our economy can afford, and far more than existing measures and efforts can cope with. Its persistence, at a time when the bulk of Canadians enjoy one of the highest standards of living in the world, is a disgrace.[36]

In the same year, the Special Senate Committee on Poverty was constituted "to investigate and report upon all aspects of poverty in Canada, …to define and elucidate the problem of poverty in Canada, and to recommend appropriate action to ensure the establishment of a more effective structure of remedial measures.[37] In addition, the war on poverty was intensified with the enactment of a new Unemployment Insurance Act in 1971, which included significantly liberalized benefits, coverage and entrance requirements; introduction and enhancement of cost-of-living indexation to OAS in 1972 and 1973; and the passage of a new Family Allowance Act in 1973, which substantially increased benefits and indexed them to the cost of living. In 1973 the National Housing Act was amended to eliminate the private profit motive in the development of social housing. It fostered the development of non-profit and cooperative housing under municipal jurisdiction and provided "a major boost to third-sector housing.[38]

The Special Senate Committee on Poverty report provides a benchmark for the profile of poverty in Canada during the sixties. Relying on Statistics Canada data for 1967, the report estimated that

> approximately 1,417,000 family units [defined by Statistics Canada as a collective term for unattached individuals and families with two or more members] had incomes below the poverty-income lines Statistics Canada had established.…In all, a total of 3,863,000 persons were described as living in poverty.…36 per cent of low-income persons were children under 16 years of age.[39]

The report challenged two popular myths about the poor. The first was the misconception that welfare recipients do not want to work. The majority of welfare recipients came from the ranks of the so-called deserving poor (those outside the labour force who could not work and were therefore considered deserving of assistance). The second myth was the general assumption that the poor are shiftless. "The poor who work— and who work hard—have been virtually ignored," the report noted. "Of the 832,000 families who, in 1967, fell below the Economic Council's poverty line, 525,000 heads of families were in the labour force—working for what can be called poverty wages."[40] In other words, in two-thirds of all poor families the head was working. To resolve the problem of poverty in Canada, the Senate Committee recommended, among other things, that "the Government of Canada implement a Guaranteed Annual Income [GAI] program" and that "full employment must be the prime objective and responsibility of government fiscal and monetary policy."[41]

Reflecting the different ideological perspectives contributing to the public discourse on poverty, a counter-report entitled The Real Poverty Report was published by four dissident staff of the Special Senate Committee who had resigned in protest.[42] The Senate poverty report, they maintained, was based on "the kind of investigation the government considers appropriate to the issue. That is, it will be useful, not as a plan for real action against inequality, but as a rough guide to the kind of thinking that created inequality in this country in the first place."[43] In contrast, their report was put forth as "an analysis of the economic system that keeps people poor."[44] In spite of the substantive differences in their explanations of the nature of poverty in Canada, however, the two reports proposed similar designs for its solution. Noting this, Haddow observes that "each advocated a comprehensive approach that would eclipse needs-tested social assistance. A GAI was to be the centrepiece in both cases, but a variety of economic policies, including the vigorous pursuit of full employment, were also seen as necessary adjuncts....The main program-related difference between the two reports pertained to benefit levels under the GAI."[45]

Table 2–3 summarizes the policy framework of the Canadian welfare state at that time, reflecting the expansion of welfare benefits under the war on poverty round.

The Canadian version of the war on poverty set in motion by the throne speech in 1965 culminated in the initiation of the Social Security Review in 1973. Release of the Working Paper on Social Security in Canada (the Orange Paper) set the terms of reference for a comprehensive federal/ provincial review of social policy. Its purpose was to determine "how best to achieve the objective of security of income for all Canadians."[46] Proposing massive income security reform, the Orange Paper "initiated the federal-provincial Social Security Review, which was known primarily for its work over three years on the design of an income supplement program for the working poor, or as it is more popularly known, a guaranteed annual income."[47] Although the review process was quickly mired down in inter-departmental and inter-governmental jurisdictional squabbles,[48] by 1975 these tensions were overshadowed and overtaken by the global economic crisis triggered by the 1973 oil embargo. Canada's economy plummeted into recession, effectively foreclosing the Liberal government's consideration of new program initiatives under the welfare state agenda and initiating a public discourse on economic crisis and fiscal restraint. In 1975, advocates of fiscal conservatism essentially took over the review agenda:

> Thereafter, the core anti-spending assumption of Finance's accumulation strategy was advanced more aggressively and successfully both by provincial treasuries and by Finance itself. This assumption was increasingly adopted by both levels of government....No government apparently challenged the conventional economic orthodoxy in Canada that in economically troubled times, the best policy was restraint and retrenchment.[49]

By the mid 1970s, the political accommodation and policy blueprint that buttressed the development of the Canadian welfare state[50] began to crack with the onset of stagflation; its neo-liberal critics—who had been consigned to the margins of political discourse in post-war reconstruction—came to the fore in the political debates of the 1970s. This was not an exclusively Canadian phenomenon. Throughout the Western world, the welfare state came under attack as high unemployment, high inflation and high public sector deficits badgered the post-industrial economies of Western nations. "The new Right is in no doubt about the source of current economic difficulties," observed a prominent student of Canadian social policy. "The policies pursued by post-war governments, legitimized by Keynesian teachings, are largely to blame for the high rates of inflation in western economies."[51] The epistemology of economic crisis dominated public discourse in the late 1970s and throughout the 1980s. So intense was the clarion call of crisis that Linda McQuaig, the noted journalist and public policy critic, observed that it was "coming from virtually all established information sources....a prevailing ideology has taken hold in our culture with a ferocity that has all but eliminated any meaningful debate."[52]

Thus, the Social Security Review of 1973 not only marks the end of the expansion of the Canadian welfare state but also the beginning of its decline. In the decade that followed, major cutbacks in Canada's social

TABLE 2–3: Policy Framework of the Canadian Welfare State, 1973

Programme	Federal Transfer Recipient	Policy
Income security:		
- Social insurance	- Unemployed	- Unemployment Insurance (1971)
- Universal	- Families with children	- Family Allowances (1973)
	- Elderly	- Old Age Security (indexed, 1973)
- Selective	- Retired, disabled workers and dependent survivors	- Canada Pension Plan (1965)
	- Provinces	- Canada Assistance Plan (1965)
	- Elderly	- Guaranteed Income Supplement (1967)
Health insurance	- Provinces	- *Health Insurance and Diagnostic Services Act* (1957)
		- *Medical Act* (1966)
Higher education	- Provinces	- *Federal-Provincial Fiscal Arrangements Act* (1967)
Housing	- Provinces and municipalities	- *National Housing Act* (amended 1964 and 1973)
Equalization	- Provinces	- Equalization payments (1957; 1967 formula revision)

safety net were initiated with reductions in Unemployment Insurance (UI) benefits (1975, 1977 and 1978) and Family Allowance (FA) benefits (1979). The Child Tax Credit, legislated in 1978, reduced the impact of changes in UI and FA by providing an income supplement to middle and low income families through the tax system, but the fundamental principle of collective risk that framed universal programs was eroded. The principle of shared risk was eroded in the cost-sharing funding formula as well. With the Federal-Provincial Fiscal Arrangements and Established Programs Financing Act of 1977 (EPF), the federal contribution to health and higher education was changed from conditional grants and 50–50 cost sharing to a combination of cash transfers and taxing power transfers to the provinces (block funds calculated on a per capita basis with no provincial spending conditions attached), in effect transferring "all the risk of rising health-care costs to the provinces."[53] In 1982, equalization payments were entrenched in the repatriated constitution under Section 36(2) of the *1982 Constitution Act*. Transfer payments, considerably downsized by revising the funding formula, were revised to a standard based on the revenue generating capacity of five designated provinces: Ontario, Quebec, Saskatchewan, Manitoba, and British Columbia. In contrast to cutbacks in other social programs, senior benefits continued to increase. For OAS, a spouse's allowance was introduced in 1975, and partial pensions based on years of residence introduced in 1977. In 1988, OAS was made taxable and an expanded spouse's allowance to all low-income widows and widowers was introduced. For CPP, full indexation was introduced and coverage expanded.

In 1984, the Canada Health Act established the principles of medicare—universality, accessibility, comprehensiveness, portability, public administration—in legislation and gave the federal government the power to withhold cash payments for medicare from the provinces or territories that failed to comply with these principles. With its passage, the federal government essentially reversed the use of its spending power from positive incentive to negative sanction as a manner of enforcing the principles of the welfare state. Then, in 1986, the federal government took unilateral action in targeting EPF for significant reductions by restricting its annual growth. The GNP escalator was decreased by two percent each year. In 1989, this cutback was increased to three percent; and in the next budget per capita EPF transfers were frozen.

Table 2–4 summarizes the tattered policy framework of the Canadian welfare state on the eve of the House of Commons resolution on child poverty.

Control of the Process of Social Policy Determination

The struggle for control over the process of social policy determination has occurred in the context of federal development. Canadian federalism, based on the constitutional division of jurisdiction and authority between the central government and ten provincial governments, can be defined as relations between federal and provincial governments. Over the course of Canadian history, Canadian federalism has changed as the role of the state in society has changed. In State, Society, and the Development of Canadian Federalism, Simeon and Robinson contrast classical federalism with modern federalism.[55] The social forces of economic development wrought immigration, urbanization and industrialization in their wake, promoting change in the size and composition of Canada's population, economy, and social institutions. Depression and war facilitated the changing role of government and the transformation from classical to modern federalism was reflective of these changes.

The form of government at the time of confederation (1867) is representative of the classical form of federalism. "The classical model implied that each order of government was sovereign and equal within its respective

TABLE 2–4: Policy Framework of the Canadian Welfare State, 1989

Program	Federal Transfer Recipient	Policy
Income security:		
- Social insurance	- Unemployed	- Unemployment Insurance (benefit reductions: 1975, 1977, 1978)
- Universal	- Families with children	- Family Allowances (benefit reductions: 1979)
	- Elderly	- Old Age Security (substantially augmented 1973-85
- Selective	- Retired, disabled workers and dependent survivors	- Canada Pension Plan (substantially augmented over time[54])
	- Provinces	- Canada Assistance Plan (1965)
	- Low income elderly	- Guaranteed Income Supplement (1967)
	- Low income families with children	- Child Tax Credit (1978) (eligibility enhanced, 1988)
Health insurance and higher education	- Provinces	- *Federal-Provincial Fiscal Arrangements and Established Programs Financing Act (1977)*
	- Provinces	- *Canada Health Act (1984)*
Housing	- Municipalities	- *National Housing Act (amended 1973)*
Equalization	- Provinces	- Equalization payments (1957; 1982 formula revision)

sphere of jurisdiction."[56] In the agricultural society of nineteenth-century Canada, the functional division of authority between regional and national matters was relatively straightforward and was not confounded by overlapping jurisdictions and conflicting mandates. By contrast, modern Canadian federalism "is distinguished from its predecessor by its thorough-going departure from the classical, 'watertight compartments' model established in the last years of the nineteenth century. Post-war federalism is characterized by much higher levels of jurisdictional overlap and policy interdependence or...'de facto concurrence' of jurisdictions."[57]

The issue of concern here is the nature of federalism as it relates to the struggle for control over the processes of social policy determination. What Simeon and Robinson called modern federalism spans the second half of the twentieth century, a period of rapid social change and a rapid transformation of the functions and roles of government. In the performance of these functions and roles, federal-provincial relations became progressively more constrained—indeed, ultimately strained—by increasingly overlapping jurisdictions and divided authority. The friction was clearly manifested within the framework of the welfare state, as federal dominance of social policy determination was its hallmark, even though the constitution assigned responsibility to the provinces:

> Major programs in the areas of health, social assistance, and post-secondary education are the product of relations between federal and provincial governments, with the programs assuming the form of complex fiscal arrangements through which the federal government offers financial assistance to the provinces. Though both federal and provincial governments have their own exclusive social programs, the welfare state in Canada has been in large part a creation of the interplay of public authorities at the federal and provincial levels.[58]

In his seminal book *The Welfare State and Canadian Federalism* (1987), Keith Banting identified three areas in which federalism influenced social policy determination in the development of the Canadian welfare state: scope, redistributive outcomes, and the balance of interests that influence policy outcomes. According to Banting, federalism's influence on scope "is clearly conservative....Divided jurisdiction is still a conservative force in welfare politics. In keeping with other forms of political fragmentation of authority, divided jurisdiction raises the level of consensus required" for policy change.[59] On federalism's impact on redistribution, Banting concluded that national income security programs functioned more to redistribute resources inter-regionally than across income groups:

> the particular structure of Canadian government has helped poor regions, not by channeling an exceptionally large proportion of our national resources into regional programs, but by transforming income security, the quintessential instrument of interpersonal redistribution, into a potent instrument of interregional redistribution.[60]

Finally, in terms of the balance of interests that influence policy outcomes, federalism bifurcated the Canadian welfare state into federal versus provincial interests. The constitutional jurisdiction and authority of the federal government is relatively remote and abstract in terms of the patterns of everyday life for most Canadians—defense, trade and commerce, weights and measures—while that of provincial governments is directly related to the patterns of everyday life—health, education, welfare. Banting argued that income security is the only direct, beneficial link between Ottawa and the public, a link that ties the interests of millions of Canadians to the strength of the federal government rather than to their provincial government....Income security is thus an important part of the federal government's capacity both to manage the economy and to maintain the allegiance of Canadians.[61]

The welfare state was a powerful instrument for nation-building in the sense that it was able to assist in constructing a sense of Canadian identity and foster an allegiance to the state.

In the framework of modern federalism, various fiscal arrangements involving the transfer of financial assistance from the federal government to the provinces were used to reconcile the gap between the responsibility assigned to the provinces for social programs and the revenue-generating capacity assigned to the federal government by the constitution. These arrangements were constitutionally justified by the authority granted to the federal government to spend in areas of provincial responsibility. The variety of fiscal arrangements utilized for social policy involved the transfer of cash and/or tax points, and included

- conditional grants requiring provinces to comply with conditions relating to program operations;
- unconditional grants;
- cost-shared grants, which reimbursed the provinces for a percentage of their expenditures in areas for which reimbursement is available; and
- bloc funding involving a transfer of a set amount of money that is unrelated to provincial expenditures in a program area.

The welfare state incorporated two distinct stages in federal-provincial relations—cooperative federalism and executive federalism.

Cooperative Federalism
The term cooperative federalism marks the character of federal-provincial relations that prevailed in the 1960s. Before "the postwar development of the Keynesian welfare state in Canada, the two levels of government in the federation had pursued their respective tasks in virtual isolation from one another."[62] In the development of a cohesive national strategy to meet the challenges posed by World War II and post-war planning, the federal role greatly expanded and intergovernmental roles became blurred. The expanded federal role conflicted with the constitution, which set out rigid boundaries of responsibility for the two levels of government. In

the framework of cooperative federalism, federal and provincial relations were marked by strong intergovernmental consultation, and decentralized agreements based on the equitable use of fiscal resources and management. The Canada Pension Plan (1965), the Medical Act (1966), and the Canada Assistance Plan (1966), legislated in this period, reflect that nature of cooperative federalism.

However, cooperative federalism, at its pinnacle in the 1960s, was extremely cluttered. There were too many civil servants making too many decisions at the federal, provincial, and at the intergovernmental levels, and increases in federal expenditures on social programs were politically unconstrained. To reestablish control over spending, policy decisions, and programming, the political executives began to unravel and reshuffle the network of activities within their respective governments. A significant portion of intergovernmental business became the responsibility of higher-level politicians, as opposed to remaining in the bureaucratic realm. The result was the formalization of "executive federalism."

Executive Federalism

Executive federalism characterized Canadian federalism from the late 1960s through the 1970s. In 1970 Donald Smiley, a leading scholar of Canadian federalism, stated: "the federal and provincial governments are now locked into a system of mutual interdependence in such a way that each level, in pursuing its objectives, will be frustrated to an intolerable degree unless some degree of intergovernmental collaboration is affected."[63] By 1980, he had already labeled the form of collaboration that had evolved as executive federalism, suggesting that it could be demarcated by looking at "the relations between elected and appointed officials of the two orders of government in federal-provincial interactions."[64] In 1981, at a Liberal Party fundraiser, Prime Minister Trudeau summed up the purpose of executive federalism by stating: "Executive federalism is characterized by the idea that the role of Parliament in governing the country should diminish while premiers should acquire more influence over national public policy. In effect, this theory means that Canada's national government would be a council of first ministers."[65]

The changes in the welfare state during this period included amendments to Family Allowance, Unemployment Insurance, Canada Pension Plan, and Old Age Security, and the inception of Child Tax Credit. The public was excluded from much of the political system's most important discussions and decisions, and executive federalism was characterized as "behind closed doors" politics. Perhaps its most infamous expression was the 1987 Meech Lake Accord on amending the Canadian Constitution. "The

38

appropriateness of the processes of executive federalism and the degree to which they bypassed deliberation in the legislatures and by the public on major constitutional issues was one of the major issues in the debate on the Meech Lake Accord."[66]

Under the welfare state framework, federal transfers to the provinces progressively increased from almost $4 billion in 1971 to over $21 billion in 1985.[67] As this reflects, executive federalism had failed in the federal government's effort to address the thorny problem of rising social spending. With the cap on the annual growth of EPF transfers, the government resorted to unilateralist action to reign in social spending. The passage of the Canada Health Act in 1984 signaled the end of federal control over the processes of social policy determination through financial incentive. Thereafter, the provinces pressed for increasing control of social policy determination, and the Canadian social safety net began to fragment as individual provinces undertook new social policy initiatives on their own. Ed Broadbent's 1989 House of Common's proposal for a resolution to eliminate child poverty may have been an effort to reinvigorate the political will to maintain a national framework for social policy,[68] but no new federal initiatives were undertaken within the Canadian welfare state framework.

3

The Residual State and the Mobilization of Charity

The concept of the residual state refers to a state's commitment to promote an ethic of liberal individualism in public policy in general, and social policy in particular. With the ideological onslaught of supply-side economics initiated in the 1980s by Prime Minister Margaret Thatcher in Britain (1979–90) and President Ronald Reagan in the United States (1981–89), the welfare state's policy blueprint[1] was readily displaced by the social forces promoting globalization. The deconstruction of the welfare state and development of the residual state ensued as a general trend across Western Europe and North America in the last quarter of the twentieth century, although the pace of the process varied from state to state.[2] This process was coterminous with the emergence of child poverty discourse, and in Canada encompassed the child poverty and child development rounds of state discourse on poverty, which bridged the transition from welfare state to residual state.

Child Poverty Round

Initiated with the 1989 House of Commons resolution on the elimination of child poverty by 2000, the child poverty round of state discourse on poverty was enveloped in a political atmosphere of national crisis—over budget deficits and national debt, the threat of Quebec separatism, and increasing federal-provincial acrimony regarding overlapping policy jurisdictions and fiscal transfers. Federal initiative in this context focused on constitutional reform and in September 1991, the government tabled in Parliament a set of proposals for the renewal of the Canadian federation that initiated widespread public and inter-governmental consultation on constitutional renewal. In August 1992 this process resulted in the formulation of the Charlottetown Accord, a proposal to substantively amend the Canadian constitution. The Accord was a multifaceted proposal for changes to the organization of the federal government and the exercise of its powers; the entrenchment of a social charter; recognition for Quebec as a distinct society and the First Nation peoples' inherent right to self-determination; and a constitutional amending formula. As it related to social policy in general—and to the problem of poverty in particular—the social charter proposed that a provision be added to the constitution describing the commitment of the governments, parliament and the legislatures within the Canadian federation to the principle of the preservation and development of Canada's social union. The objectives of the social union, the Accord proposed, should not be justifiable and should include:[3]

- Providing throughout Canada a health care system that is comprehensive, universal, portable, publicly administered and accessible;
- Providing adequate social services and benefits to ensure that all individuals resident in Canada have reasonable access to housing, food, and other basic necessities;
- Providing high quality primary and secondary education to all individuals resident in Canada and ensuring reasonable access to post-secondary education;
- Protecting the rights of workers to organize and bargain collectively; and,
- Protecting, preserving and sustaining the integrity of the environment for present and future generations.

Essentially the Charlottetown Accord proposed to constitutionally entrench the principles of the Canadian welfare state, in effect reflecting that in a political process based on a consensus model these principles prevailed. However, in a national referendum on October 26, 1992, the Charlottetown Accord was rejected in six provinces and the Yukon, largely due to widespread public resistance to constitutional recognition of Quebec as a distinct society. Following this in December 1992, and in sharp contrast to the universal safety net approach advanced by the Charlottetown Accord, the Conservative government initiated the child poverty approach with the abolition of the Canadian welfare state's first universal program, Family Allowances. It was replaced with the income-tested Child Tax Benefit, which consolidated the refundable and non-refundable Child Tax Credit.

A federal election in 1993 replaced the Progressive Conservative government with a Liberal government—constitutional reform was off the national agenda as a solution to the problems facing the Canadian federation. In January 1994 the government announced a multifaceted review and reform of social security. The objectives of this review provide a sharp contrast with the social objectives outlined in the Charlottetown Accord:

- Jobs—helping Canadians get and keep work by ensuring that we have the knowledge and skills to compete with the best labour forces in the world.
- Support for those most vulnerable—providing income support for those in need, while fostering independence, self-confidence and initiative, and starting to tackle child poverty.
- Affordability—making sure the social security system is within our means and more efficiently managed, with a real commitment to end waste and abuse.[4]

Through the spring and summer of 1994, the Ministry of National Health and Welfare's Standing Committee on Human Resources Development held extensive public hearings on social security reform with the commitment that Parliamentary consideration of actual legislation would take place in the fall or early in the New Year. Task force groups were organized and town hall meetings were held throughout Canada. However, the entire process appeared to be a boondoggle as the 1995 federal budget preempted the review process by making massive cuts in transfer payments to the provinces. The Canada Assistance Plan (CAP), Canada's most recent cost-shared program, was terminated along with Established Programs Financing (EPF), and the Canada Health and Social Transfer (CHST) was introduced in their place.

The CHST constituted an unconditional grant to the provinces for health, social welfare and post-secondary education. With its introduction, the federal government

> eliminated two of the rules governing the administration of social assistance programs funded by federal transfers. There is no longer a requirement that these programs be made available to all in need. Furthermore, provinces are no longer required to provide an appeal process for those denied assistance....As under EPF, there are no conditions attached to the postsecondary education services funded by the grant. Finally, in the transition from two programs to one, the federal government removed approximately $2.5 billion of funding that would have otherwise been made available during the fiscal year 1996–97 and approximately $4.5 billion in 1997–98, producing a total transfer of 26.9 billion in 1996–97 and $25.1 billion in 1997–98.[5]

With the 1995 budget, the federal government dismantled the last vestige of its role as architect of social policy in Canada. In 1996, the last plank in the Canadian welfare state framework—and arguably its fundamental anti-poverty program—was dismantled with the replacement of the Unemployment Insurance Act with the Employment Insurance Act (EI), which provided very restrictive benefits, coverage, and entrance requirements. EI in effect disenfranchised large segments of the Canadian labour force from protection against impoverishment due to the exigencies and contingencies of the labour market in a changing capitalist economy. Reflecting the shift from welfare state to residual state ethic, federal social policy portfolios were reorganized in 1996, the Ministry of National Health and Welfare disappeared, and the Ministry of Human Resources Development (HRDC) was created.[6]

With the final coup de grace delivered to the Canadian welfare state, the framework for intergovernmental relations in the residual state was put in place with the creation of the Federal-Provincial-Territorial Council (F/P/T) on Social Policy Renewal in 1996. Composed of first ministers from nine provinces (Quebec declined membership) and both territories, and co-chaired by the minister of HRDC and a provincial first minister, the new council assumed the mandate to direct and guide the development of "a new partnership to renew Canada's social safety net," and established its first priorities to be children in low-income families and persons with disabilities.[7] The social safety net, in other words, was to be a net for the deserving poor—those unable to compete in the labour market. Given the high profile of child poverty on the national agenda since the 1989 House resolution, it received priority attention in the residual state. In February 1997, the federal budget announced an initial and ongoing federal commitment of $600 million for a National Child Benefit (NCB) in cooperation with the provinces and territories. Consistent with the ideological spin of liberal individualism, following the budget speech, the F/P/T emphasized that the goals of the NCB were to reduce child poverty, promote workforce attachment, and reduce overlap and duplication.[8]

F/P/T initiative in the area of disability followed. In October 1997, it approved a Multilateral Framework for Employability Assistance for People with Disabilities (EAPD). Consistent with the residual state's neo-liberal ethic, the EAPD replaced the Vocational Rehabilitation for Disabled Persons (VRDP) program with a much stronger emphasis on employability. The VRDP program had been in place since 1962 and reflected the social needs ethic of the welfare state era. In sharp contrast, the EAPD reflected the F/P/T's harmonization strategy for income support and its goal of reducing barriers to work inherent in income support programs—that is, to work in the low-paid insecure jobs without benefits that were rapidly displacing well-paid jobs with benefits in the globalizing labour market. Under the EAPD, the federal government agreed to contribute up to a maximum of 50 percent of the cost of eligible provincial/territorial programs and services designed to "help people with disabilities prepare for, obtain and maintain employment."[9] Eligible costs "provide the skills, experience and related supports necessary to prepare people with disabilities for economic participation and employment in the labour market."[10]

The NCB and EADP represented the first social policy initiatives under the residual state framework, and their passage in effect signaled state closure on the child poverty round. Portrayed as a partnership among governments, they looked more like a parasitic relationship with the federal government as the financial host supporting provincial downsizing of social allowance programs. In fact, the linkage between provincial social allowance programs and federal financing was explicit with the NCB. Under the NCB, the federal government agreed to provide low-income families with a supplement to the Child Tax Benefit—the base benefit received by over 80 percent of Canadian families with children. The provinces in turn were to reduce social allowance payments by a commensurate amount and re-invest the savings in programs "to reduce the welfare wall by providing child benefits outside of welfare and ensuring that enhanced benefits and services continue when parents move from social assistance to paid employment."[11] Examples of provincial reinvestment plans included extending health benefits to low-income families with children, increased support for child care, early intervention services, and training programs for low-income families with children.[12] While no family receiving provincial social assistance was to experience a reduction in its overall level of income support as a result of the NCB, in fact most provinces used NCB to justify cutting back welfare rolls to promote work attachment. Between March 1997 and March 1999, the number of Canadian welfare recipients declined from 2,774,900 to 2,279,100.[13] Not surprisingly, the two provinces with the most strident ideological commitment to liberal individualism at the time—Ontario and Alberta—registered the highest proportional cutbacks in welfare rolls: 21 and 20 percent respectively while the provincial average was 14 percent.

45

Child Development Round

The child poverty round of Canadian social policy development, initiated with the 1989 House of Commons resolution, culminated with the passage of the NCB in 1997, and child development replaced child poverty on the residual state agenda. With state discourse on child development already well-advanced by 1997,[14] the transition was seamless. In September 1997, the Government of Canada announced in the Speech from the Throne the National Children's Agenda (NCA), a framework for the federal, provincial, and territorial governments "to work together to develop. . .a comprehensive strategy to improve the well-being of Canada's children."[15] Under the aegis of the F/T/P, public consultations were initiated. Over the spring and summer of 1999, Aboriginal organizations, children and youth service agencies, and non-governmental organizations participated in roundtable discussions and focus group forums organized by federal, provincial, and territorial governments to reframe public discourse from child poverty to child development—essentially promoting a utilitarian vision of happy, healthy children.[16]

With the residual state initiated, in March 1998 the F/T/P began negotiations to formalize "a new partnership approach between governments in the planning and managing of Canada's social union" based on "collaborative approaches on the use of the federal spending power."[17] Negotiations concluded with the signing of the Social Union Framework Agreement (SUFA) on February 4, 1999. Like the Canada Assistance Program (CAP)—the framework for intergovernmental relations in the provision of social programs in the welfare state—SUFA provided the framework for social program provision in the residual state. In contrast to CAP, the provinces, rather than the federal government, were the architects of SUFA. And unlike CAP, SUFA was "more about process—about how governments should relate to one another and to their citizens in the making of social policy—than it is about substantive new social policy commitments."[18] Cast in general terms, SUFA did little more than outline provincial commitments to general principles of equality and accessibility in the provision of services, and to accountability, transparency and collaboration in their administration. Beyond the loose commitments, SUFA placed constraints on the federal role vis-à-vis social programs, particularly the use of federal spending power, to operate within the limits of constitutional jurisdictions. Specifically, with regard to cost-shared and block-funded social programs, the federal government agreed to "consult with provincial and territorial governments at least one year prior to renewal or significant funding changes to existing social transfers" and not to introduce new initiatives "without the agreement of a majority of provincial governments."[19] With regard to direct federal transfers to individuals and organizations for health care, post-secondary education, social assistance, and social services, the federal government agreed to give provincial/territorial governments "at least three months' notice [prior to implementation] and offer to consult."[20]

In essence, SUFA provided a framework for the federal government to record Canadian Health and Social Transfer (CHST) payments to provinces, and for the provinces to report on the social programs subsidized by CHST transfers. As an umbrella for Canadian social policy, SUFA replaced the development of a national social safety net for Canadians with the pursuit of instrumental intergovernmental relations in the provincial development of a social service employment trampoline. That is, the social safety net was superceded by a framework of social services designed to bounce people back into the labour market—the legitimate mode of needs satisfaction in liberal individualism. SUFA also fundamentally limited the scope of state responsibility for the social welfare of citizens to the deserving poor, defined in terms of services to the disabled and to children. Although framed earlier, the EADP, NCB, and NCA all fell under the SUFA canopy.

Additional agreements followed that focused on services to children under six and their families and services to the disabled. In September 2000, the F/T/P added the Early Childhood Development Agreement (ECD). Under its terms, the federal government agreed to transfer $2.2 billion over five years through the CHST to provincial and territorial governments "to support their investments in early childhood development programs and services in four key areas—promoting healthy pregnancy, birth and infancy; improving parenting and family supports; strengthening early childhood development, learning and care; and strengthening community supports."[21] Consistent with the child development frame, the provinces promoted a variety of health, education and child care programs targeted at young children in general, vulnerable children in particular.[22] The array of services available varied from province to province[23] as CHST investments were based on provincial priorities, not national standards. In addition to providing fiscal support for provincial and territorial programs in the area of ECD, the federal government was also involved in the direct provision of early childhood development programs to First Nation and Inuit populations, and for children and families at risk (a euphemism for families living in poverty). These included the Community Action Program for Children, which funds community-based coalitions to establish and deliver services to children at risk; and the Canada Prenatal Nutrition Program for pregnant women at risk.[24]

In March 2003, the F/T/P approved the Multilateral Framework on Early Learning and Child Care to "support the participation of parents in employment or training by improving access to affordable, quality early learning and child care programs and services."[25] Under its terms, the federal government agreed to transfer $900 million over five years to provincial and territorial governments through the CHST for investments in

47

direct care and early learning settings such as child care centres, family child care homes, preschools and nursery schools. Types of investments that will be made under this framework include capital and operating funding, fee subsidies, wage enhancements, training, professional development and support, quality assurance, and parent information and referral.[26]

In addition to providing fiscal support for provincial and territorial early learning and child care programs, the federal government also provided funding for the delivery of early learning and child care programs to First Nation and Inuit populations, and for Aboriginal Head Start programs for aboriginal children at risk living in some urban and northern communities.

Thus, the social union in the residual state both restricted the scope of state responsibility for social welfare and subordinated federal spending power in the social policy area to provincial jurisdiction. A federal-provincial division of labour in the provision of public welfare benefits emerged. Under SUFA, the federal role is limited to the delivery of income support to the needy (labeled at risk in federal policy discourse) through a pauperized social safety net. Provincial responsibility centres on labour force attachment related services to vulnerable children and the disabled. While SUFA established the public dimension of welfare benefits in the residual state, the Voluntary Sector Initiative (VSI), launched in June 2000, prepared the groundwork for mobilizing the private sector of voluntary services. VSI kicked off a five-year joint initiative between the federal government and the voluntary sector, "focused on strengthening the relationship between the sector and the government and enhancing the capacity of the voluntary sector" to respond to social problems and community needs.[27] In essence, the VSI signaled the culmination of the general trend initiated in the late 1970s of "increasing public provision of social services through the private sector,"[28] and, conversely, the initiation of private provision through the public sector. Designed to stimulate private sector provision of social services to the marginalized and disadvantaged, the VSI essentially promised fiscal support to the voluntary sector for the development of social services, and initiated a two-phase process. In its initial phase, from June 2000 to October 2002, 23 representatives from the voluntary sector were brought together to form a Voluntary Sector Steering Group (VSSG). The VSSG worked with representatives of the federal government to frame an accord that would govern the relationship between the two sectors. The accord,[29] drafted in 2001, established the framework for federal-voluntary sector collaboration. This was followed with the drafting of codes of conduct—the Codes of Good Practice—to regulate practice around policy dialogue and funding. Implementation and evaluation were to take place in the second phase, scheduled to run from November 2002 to March 2005.

Thus, in place of the public social safety net of the welfare state, the residual state presented Canadians in the twenty-first century with the vision of a voluntary net of community services. Table 3–1 summarizes the

TABLE 3–1: Policy Framework for the Residual State, 2003

Programme	Federal Transfer Recipient	Policy
Income support programs	- Unemployed workers	- Employment Insurance (1996)
	- Retired, disabled workers and dependent survivors	- Canada Pension Plan (1965 and successive augmentations)
	- Elderly	- Old Age Security (1952; 1975 and 1988 modifications)
	- Low income elderly	- Guaranteed Income Supplement (1967)
	- Moderate and low-income families with children	- Canadian Child Tax Benefit (1978; 1997 modification)
	- Low-income families with children	- National Child Benefit (1997)
	- Working parents	- Child Care Expense Deduction (1971, increased 1998)
Health and higher education	Provinces	- Canada Health and Social Transfer (1995; 2003 modification)
Social Services[149]	- Voluntary sector	- Voluntary Sector Initiative (2000)
Equalization	- Provinces	- Equalization grants (1957; 1982 formula revision)
	- Provinces (via CHST)	- Multilateral Framework for Employability Assistance for People with Disabilities (1997)
	- Provinces (via CHST)	- Early Childhood Development Agreement (2000)
	- Provinces (via CHST)	- Multilateral Framework on Early Learning and Child Care (2003)

policy framework of the Canadian residual state that had emerged by 2003.

Income security (covering income support, maintenance and replacement) and basic needs programs (housing, education, health) represented the central pillars of social policy under the welfare state model. During its evolution (1940–73), these programs progressively expanded their coverage; during its devolution (1974–97), they were progressively contracted. In contrast, the central pillars of social policy under the residual state model appear to be programs related to equalization of provincial capacities to offer comparable social service programs for children and the disabled, and to the mobilization of voluntary programs. The income maintenance and replacement functions of income security have been pauperized, and income support harmonized with the "less eligibility" principle that maintains public support below minimum wage standards.

Significance of Child Poverty

As discussed in Chapter One, facts about child poverty indicate meaning and significance, and in the transition from welfare state to residual state, measures and meanings in state discourse were systematically modified to reflect changing ideological perspectives. However, this transition begs for consideration of the measured and unmeasured effects of poverty on childhood. As Table 1–4 reflects, however measured poverty is a reality for some proportion of Canadian children. What does it mean to grow up poor in Canada? Poverty has both relative and absolute dimensions. The relative dimension relates to standard of living, which constitutes a powerful cultural symbol and has potent subjective and inter-subjective meanings in the context of an advanced market economy. Income is the primary determinant of standard of living, and the quintile distribution of family income provides an indicator of the relative standing of families in the labour market competition for income. The quintiles rank income groups in the population from lowest to highest share of total family income, and these ranks roughly correspond to popular notions of lower, working, middle and upper classes. Chart 3–1, "Percentage Distribution of Family Income by Total Income Quintiles," provides an indication of the income of poor families in comparison to non-poor families.

The relative stability of total income distribution across the five quintiles over the course of the 45-year period reflected in Chart 3–1 is striking in the context of phenomenal growth in the Canadian economy. Between 1961 and 1971, Canada's GDP increased by more than 50 percent to over $276 billion; by 1996, it had increased to $617.5 billion.[32] The role of the welfare state, in fact, was to stabilize income distribution, not to change it, and welfare state programs were largely financed by economic growth, not by vertical income redistribution. In effect, economic growth shielded the standard of living of wealthy and middle classes from the burden of income redistribution, while the welfare state stabilized the standard of living of the working and middle classes.[33] With the economic recession of the early 1970s, the ideological foundation of the shield began to erode. Research on the impact of poverty on childhood is under funded in Canada, and as a result evidence appears to be more anecdotal than systematic. Nevertheless, there is sufficient research in comparable jurisdictions—

CHART 3–1: Percentage Distribution of Family Income by Total Income Quintiles, Selected Years, 1951–1996 and After-tax Income Quintiles, 1993–2002[31]

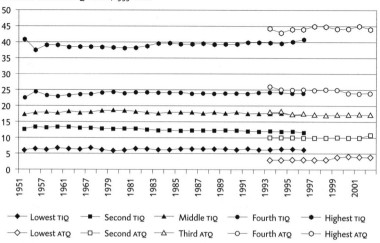

the United States and United Kingdom for example—to substantiate the deleterious impact of poverty on child health and give credence to anecdotal reports.[34] Canadian reports indicate that poor children are at higher risk of poor health than non-poor children. The quality of nutrition is directly affected by income and impacts on the health of a child even before its birth. Dietary deficiencies in expectant mothers increase the likelihood of prenatal and perinatal mortality or pre-maturity. The final report of the Standing Senate Committee on Social Affairs, Science and Technology—the Marsden report, submitted in January 1991—cited evidence submitted by the Canadian Medical Association and the Ontario Medical Association to conclude that:

> The incidence of low birth weight, the single most important cause of infant mortality and a common predecessor of poor health in childhood and later life, is also higher among poor mothers. …the significance of good nutrition for pregnant and breast-feeding mothers cannot be over-emphasized. For example, children born to poor parents generally weigh 200–300 grams less than infants born to their better-off counterparts.[35]

The effects of poverty on infants are mediated through low birth weight, which greatly increases a child's risk for a host of health problems in early and later stages of life. "Over the longer term, these same infants run greater risks of mental deficiencies, physical handicaps, slow or retarded growth and neuromotor problems."[36] Malnutrition contributes to developmental delay, which may in turn contribute to "generational poverty."[37] According to Statistics Canada's National Longitudinal Survey of Children and Youth (NLSCY) launched in 1994:

> During the first three years of life, children's brains and nervous systems are growing and developing, and they are acquiring language, motor and social skills. A good foundation for healthy child development thus depends largely upon the mother's health and health habits during her pregnancy.[38]

52

The connection between poverty and health is not mysterious. The lack of financial resources leads to poor diets. Poor nutrition is a precursor to poor health, especially for children. Because poor families generally cannot afford to feed their family on a nutritious diet of quality protein and fresh fruits and vegetables, they rely on low cost diets that are high in carbohydrates and sugars. In a 1991 report on child poverty, the Social Planning Council of Metropolitan Toronto cited reports that noted that such diets put children at risk because "poor nutrition undermines children's resistance to infectious diseases....Twice as many low-income children are likely to suffer from chronic health problems than are non-poor children."[39]

The links between income and nutritional health are significant, and for poor families social assistance cutbacks have made access to food tenuous. The Marsden report noted that for many low income families, particularly those living on social assistance, "the food budget is very often the 'catch-all' budget. In other words, non-food expenses which cannot be met are often subsidized by the food dollar."[40] In 1992, a Statistics Canada study reported that families with children, particularly families on social assistance and the working poor, were the most dependent on food banks. In 1991, about two million people, including 700,000 children under 18 years of age, received assistance from food banks. According to Oderkirk:[41]

> Children are over represented among those receiving food relief. According to the Canadian Association of Food Banks in 1990, children under age 18 accounted for about 40% of food bank beneficiaries. However, only 25% of Canada's total population were children that age. In 1990, one out of every nine children under age 18 received emergency food assistance from the food bank an average of 3.5 times per year. Also, families with children received two-thirds of the 3.2 million grocery baskets distributed in Canada that year.[42]

Similarly, a 1998 Hunger Count survey by the Canadian Association of Food Banks (CAFB) reported that 41.5 percent of food bank recipients in 1997 were children.[43]

Reflecting on the 1998 survey, the CAFB concluded "food bank use doubled from 1989 to 1997, and then grew by 5.4 percent from 1997 to 1998. This situation is particularly disturbing. Even in a period of economic growth, hunger continues to increase throughout Canada."[44] A more systematic examination of the problem of child hunger in Canada was undertaken by Human Resources Development Canada. Based on a careful analysis of data from the National Longitudinal Survey of Children and Youth, a strategic policy working paper prepared for the department concluded that:

53

> Frequent or long episodes of hunger can have harmful and long term effects on the health and development of the child. Hunger, a consequence of extreme disadvantage, was experienced by...57,000 Canadian families with children. Single parent families, families on social assistance and Aboriginal families are over-represented. One-third of the families...[are] the working poor. Hunger was a problem that co-occurred with the mother's poor health and activity limitations. The difference in annual income between those who experience frequent hunger and those who experience occasional hunger is $5000.[45]

In 1975, a Nutrition Canada survey reported a lower protein diet among mothers in low-income categories.[46] Not only are higher protein foods too expensive for low-income earners, the survey also indicated a lower intake of all nutrients among women from lower income groups. NLSCY identifies low income as a health risk factor for all children, not only expectant mothers. One in four Canadian children under age 12 lived in low-income families in 1994.[47] The nature of the risk relates more to disabilities than to infectious disease. Childhood morbidity and mortality rates have been greatly reduced over the course of the century as a result of improvements in neonatal care, public hygiene, and mass immunization programs that protect children from infectious disease. "As a result, disabilities have replaced infectious disease as the most challenging health problems incurred by children."[48] The proportion of Canadian children under age 15 with disabilities increased from 5 percent in 1986 to 7 percent in 1991 (representing 389,400 children).[49] The most common chronic health conditions affecting Canadian children in 1991 were allergies, learning disabilities, asthma, bronchitis, and behavioural or emotional difficulties.[50] The link between disabilities and poverty is clear according to Statistics Canada's 1991 Health and Activity Limitation Survey (HALS):

In general, incidence of disability is higher among children and youth under age 20 living in families with the lowest incomes than those in families with higher incomes. The reported disability rate for young people from families with the lowest incomes (8%) in 1986 was over twice as high as that for those from high-income families (4%) when the population of children and youth with disabilities was divided into quintiles by family income. The differential was even greater among the most severely disabled young people. The rate of severe disability for every 1,000 children and youth was five times higher for those families with the lowest incomes (3.0 per 1,000) than for those from families with the highest incomes (0.6 per 1,000).[51]

Poor children are not only at a higher risk of poor health than non-poor children, they are also reportedly at a higher risk of mortality. A 1990 Canadian Teachers' Federation report on child poverty prepared for the Campaign 2000 initiative maintained that:[52]

- The infant mortality rate is 2.5 times higher for the poorest area of Toronto than for the wealthiest. For Canada as a whole, it is 1.9 times higher.
- Death from birth defects is 1.5 times higher among the poor.
- Death from infectious disease is 2.5 times higher.
- Death from accidents is twice as common among poor children.
- Low birth weight babies are twice as common among the poor as among the wealthy.
- Prematurity is also more common.

4

Child Poverty and Changing Federal Policy

In discussing the significance of child poverty at the end of Chapter Three, the question of what it means to grow up poor in Canada was posed. For children who grow up in the 40 percent of Canadian families who fall into the lowest and second quintiles of income distribution, however, the question of what it means to grow up poor and near-poor reflects the larger reality of daily life. This chapter examines the relationship between child poverty and changing federal social policy in the context of this larger reality.

Child Poverty in Context

Placed in the context of income distribution, child poverty statistics represent only the tip of the proverbial iceberg. Such statistics are snapshots in time; submerged below their surface are the movements of Canadian families throughout any given year into and out of poverty—poverty dynamics. What does it mean to grow up in a family that lives in the crux of this dynamic? Research on poverty dynamics indicate that:[1]

- poverty is a revolving door for about 60 percent of those who are poor in any given year, and for the remaining forty percent poverty is a persistent state (lasting five or more years);
- for non-poor families, the risk of falling into poverty in any one year is greater the closer they are in the income distribution pyramid to the poverty line;
- the probability of exiting poverty diminishes with length of stay;
- the risk of poverty is significantly higher for young families (families with breadwinners under 35 years of age);
- single-parent families are at a greater risk of persistent poverty than two-parent families with two income earners;

• change in family breadwinner's employment status is the major factor explaining children's entry into poverty status, and change in family status (i.e., divorce) is the secondary event.

Clearly the dynamic of family life for many children—many more than indicated by poverty statistics—revolves around the risk of poverty. According to Statistics Canada, there were 8,394,000 families in Canada in 1997, and 40 percent of them (3,357,600) had incomes below $41,687, the upper income limit of the second quintile. As reflected in Table 4–1 below, LICOs vary by family size and community size, while average family income does not. That is, a family with an income of $19,100 (the average family income in the lowest quintile in 1997) may have no children, two children, four children, or more, and may or may not live in a rural community, an urban centre, or somewhere in-between. While their income does not vary by these factors, whether or not they qualify as poor does.

LICOs and the average income for the first and second quintile reflect how close the remaining 26 percent of the families in these two income quintiles are to the poverty line. In the context of changes in the Canadian labour market since NAFTA, employment has become a revolving door for a large segment of the Canadian labour force. These changes include the loss of full-time jobs with benefits in the manufacturing sector, an increase in part-time jobs without benefits in the service sector, a transition from secure long-term employment to limited-term employment, and the replacement of jobs related to information management with innovations in information technology. Particularly vulnerable to job insecurity and the risk of poverty in the residual state are young families, the family unit for a majority of young children.

Changing Federal Social Policy

Changes in federal social policy can be tracked in terms of changing patterns of expenditure on social policy, as expenditures are concrete markers or indicators of a course of action in the policy sphere. Programs categorized under federal transfer payments to persons and to other levels of government in National Income and Expenditure Accounts track federal expenditures annually. Appendix tables D–2 and D–3 identify the programs used in the calculation here of annual federal expenditures on social policy. In Table 4–2, linear regression is used to explore the relationship between child poverty and federal expenditures on social policy over two distinct time periods. The years from 1971 to 1981 mark the period of welfare state maturity ending with the onset of the 1981 to 1983 recession when the cuts

TABLE 4–1: Average Family* After-tax Income and LICO Cut-offs, 1997–2001

Year	LICO Cut-offs*	Average Income**	
		First Quintile**	Second Quintile**
1997	11,501–37,388	$19,100	$33,900
1998	11,608–37,735	$19,800	$35,000
1999	11,817–38,416	$20,600	$36,300
2000	12,138–39,459	$20,800	$37,000
2001	12,448–40,468	$22,400	$38,600
2002	12,726–41,372	$22,300	$39,000

*Economic families, two or more persons after tax
**After tax
Source: Low Income Cut-offs After Tax, 1992 Base; Rural Areas; 2 Persons from CANSIM II Table 2020801
Series V25745045. Low Income Cut-offs After Tax, 1992 Base; Urban Areas, Population 500,000 +; 7
Persons+ from CANSIM II Table 2020801 Series V25745106. Income data from Statistics Canada, Income in
Canada, 2002, cat. no. 75–202–XIE.

to UI of the late 1970s registered on income; the years from 1985 to 1995 mark the period of transition from welfare state to residual state.

The probability statistics cited in Table 4–2 indicate that the linear regression model is a good fit for both periods. In the 1971–81 period, there is less than a 0.001 chance of error in the specification of the variation in child poverty on federal expenditures; in 1985–95, there is less than 0.003 chance of error. More directly to the point of policy, the R^2s indicate the strength of the models—with 96.1 percent of variation in child poverty explained by variation in federal expenditures on social policy in the welfare state period, and only 63.7 percent explained in the residual state period. In other words, these R^2s reflect the significance of the national social safety net approach to social policy in addressing child poverty versus the targeted approach of the residual state.

The slope coefficient reflects the direction of the relationship between child poverty and federal expenditures on social policy, and the average amount of change in federal expenditures from one year to the next to cause a change in child poverty. The welfare state period indicates a negative relationship between federal expenditures and child poverty, demonstrating that child poverty decreased as federal expenditures increased. The slope of -0.074 suggests that for every $1,000,000,000 increase in federal expenditure, the number of children living in low-income families decreased by 74,000. Between 1971 and 1981, federal expenditures increased from $33,333,330,000 constant dollars to $52,317,490,000—an increase of 36.3 percent. In the same period, child poverty decreased from 2,574,000 to 1,073,000—a decrease of 58.3 percent. In contrast, the slope coefficient for the transition period points to a positive relationship between federal expenditure and child poverty, indicating that the number of children living in low-income families increased even as federal expenditures increased. The slope of 0.026 suggests that for every $1,000,000,000 increase in federal expenditure, child poverty increased by 26,000. Between 1985 and 1995, federal expenditure increased from $67,548,000,000 (constant dollars) to $74,560,460,000, an increase of 9.4 percent. In this same period, child poverty increased from 1,240,000 to 1,389,000, an increase of 10.7 percent.

As a tool of exploratory analysis, regression analysis provides support for an argument advocating the maintenance of a strong national social safety net. It is likely that both cutbacks in federal social policy expenditures and increases in child poverty were caused by the same complex processes of economic change and ideological change that have transformed the political economy of Canada over the last quarter century. In this context, it seems likely that the relationship between government expenditures and poverty is more complex than a simple exploratory model might be able to reflect. Government expenditures are a significant part of the Canadian economy. Federal expenditures on social policy, in other words, reflect not only the changing political nature of federalism but also its changing economic nature. Nevertheless, regression is a powerful exploratory tool that identifies the negative relationship between federal expenditures on social policy and child poverty in the welfare state period, and the positive relationship in the transition period.

Aggressive anti-poverty programming was enacted in the early 1970s: the new Unemployment Inusrance Act of 1971 significantly liberalized benefits, coverage and entrance requirements; the Family Allowance Act in 1973 increased benefits and indexed them to the consumer price index; and in 1972, 1973 and 1975 changes to the Old Age Security Program significantly increased coverage and indexed benefits to cost-of-living. Following these aggressive initiatives, child poverty declined from 2,574,000 in 1971 to 968,000 in 1980—a 62.4 percent decrease. In this same period, FESP per capita increased from $15.43 to $22.02 per person. By 1984, however, child poverty increased by 26.9 percent over its 1980 level. The increase in child poverty was catalyzed the 1981–83 recession, which followed major cutbacks to social programs initiated in the later half of the 1970s, including the 1975, 1977 and 1978 amendments to UI, and the 1977 passage of EPF. In effect, when the 1981–83 recession hit, the proverbial holes in the social safety net were already too large to catch the fallout.

Due to declines in the unemployment rate from 11.3 in 1984 to 7.5 in 1989, child poverty declined in that time period from 1,325,000 to 907,000—a decline of 31.5 percent. FESP per capita in this period decreased from $25.55

TABLE 4–2: Linear Regression of CP on FESP for Two Periods, 1971–81 and 1985–95

	Periods	
	Welfare State 1971–81	**Transition To Residual State 1985–95**
Probability	.001	.003
R^2	.961	.637
Slope Coefficient	-.074	.026

to $25.19. Thereafter, unemployment increased from 7.5 in 1989 to a high of 11.2 in 1993; child poverty increased substantially from its low of 907,000 in 1989 to 1,389,000 in 1995—an increase of 34.7 percent in the seven year period. In this same period, federal expenditures on social policy increased from $24.64 per capita to $26.11 per capita. In the welfare state, increases in federal expenditures precipitated declines in child poverty; under the residual state, increases in federal expenditures accompany increases in child poverty.

Child Poverty in the Residual State

By the initiation of the twenty-first century, the relationship between federal and provincial social policy had been turned on its head with the foundation of the residual state. In other words, in contrast to the architect role of federal social policy under the welfare state, in the residual state federal social policy essentially plays a handmaiden role to provincial social policy regimes. As a result, the national character of the Canadian social safety net has dissipated as each province and territory developed its own distinctive set of policies and programs, and the social benefits available to Canadians vary from province to province. Thus, the benefits in-kind and in-cash available to families with children have become dependent upon their place of residency. Table 4–3 identifies the distribution of child poverty by province in 2001.

At the provincial level, the shift from welfare state to residual state reflected welfare roll cutbacks between 1995 and 2003, as reflected in Table 4–4. The residual state framework promotes an ethic of liberal individualism—that is, work attachment and individual self-reliance—in social policy that is especially reflected at the provincial level in social assistance policies. However, the degree to which this ideologically modeled ethic is promoted throughout the social policy sphere at the provincial level varies across the provinces. Following is a review of provincial social policies under the residual Canadian state as they relate to child poverty. The review

TABLE 4–3: Children aged 17 and under living in low-income economic families (2000 income) as a proportion of all children aged 17 and under living in economic families, Canada, provinces, territories, health regions and peer groups, 2001

	Total # of children living	# of children living in low income families	the proportion of children living in low income families
Canada	6,765,105	1,229,005	18.2
Newfoundland and Labrador	111,710	26,145	23.4
Prince Edward Island	32,570	4,515	13.9
Nova Scotia	198,410	39,005	19.7
New Brunswick	157,330	28,225	17.9
Quebec	1,544,560	309,340	20.0
Ontario	2,672,615	451,195	16.9
Manitoba	252,285	52,595	20.8
Saskatchewan	230,580	43,830	19.0
Alberta	722,710	109,845	15.2
British Columbia	842,335	164,315	19.5

1. Data source: Statistics Canada, 2001 Census (20% sample).
2. Children aged 17 and under living in economic families with incomes below the Statistics Canada low-income cut-offs (LICOs).
3. The LICOs represent levels of income where people spend disproportionate amounts of money for food, shelter, and clothing.
4. LICOs are based on family and community size; cut-offs are updated to account for changes in the Consumer Price Index.
5. The term economic family refers to a group of two or more persons who live in the same dwelling and are related to each other by blood, marriage, common-law or adoption.
6. LICO data exclude institutional residents.

is organized in terms of programs extant in 2004, and describes four policy areas related to the social welfare of low-income families: income security, social housing, child care, and health care.

British Columbia

Income Security

British Columbia maintains a basic Income Assistance Program (IAP) "to assist people temporarily while they find work, and to assist those who are unable to fully participate in the workforce."[2] The underlying objective of IAP is to provide support in both cash and kind to British Columbians in a manner that encourages "personal responsibility and active participation" in seeking sustainable employment and ultimately full independence.[3] Clients are assessed as either "expected to work" (services and income assistance provided are considered, generally, short term) or "temporarily

TABLE 4–4: Change in Number of People on Welfare Between 1995 and 2003, by Province

Province	Number of People on Welfare		Percent Change
	1995	2004	
Alberta	113,200	57,800	-48.9
British Columbia	374,300	180,700	-51.7
Manitoba	85,200	59,900	-29.7
New Brunswick	67,400	49,300	-26.8
Newfoundland	71,300	51,200	-28.2
Nova Scotia	104,000	58,300	-43.9
Ontario	1,344,600	673,900	-49.9
PEI	12,400	7,000	-43.5
Quebec	802,200	544,200	-32.2
Saskatchewan	82,200	53,200	-35.3

Source: National Council of Welfare, Welfare Incomes, 2003, Vol. #121.

excused" (assistance provided where unusual circumstances, such as a medical condition, are a barrier to employment). Eligibility is means tested and includes a test that requires applicants to demonstrate that they have been financially independent for at least two consecutive years. In addition, employable Income Assistance clients are limited to a cumulative 24 months of assistance out of every 60 months.[4] Because the primary objective of British Columbia's IAP is to focus on getting and keeping clients in the work force, these time limits were implemented as a caution to applicants to actively seek employment, services and support elsewhere—from family, friends and within their communities. Both the IAP's time limit and two-year independence constraints include criteria that exempt, for example, persons with disabilities, pregnant women and categories of refugees.

Other financial benefits provided to help low and moderate income families with children include the BC Family Bonus and BC Earned Income Benefit programs. The Earned Income Benefit is fully funded by the province and administered by the Canada Revenue Agency. Financial benefits are available to low-income seniors through the Seniors Supplement Program (payable to couples only), and the Hardship Assistance Program (benefits are time-limited and dependent on employment profile). Benefits in "kind" for those eligible for IAP include bus passes for seniors, transportation for disabled persons, as well as items required to stay in the work force, such as work boots and safety clothing.

BC's Ministry of Human Resources (MHR) provides a number of employment-focused subprograms to low-income residents, including

Community Assistance, Training For Jobs, Job Placement and the Employment Program for Persons with Disabilities. The Ministry also offers a Bridging Employment program to assist IAP recipients gain employment. This program targets women fleeing abuse, former sex trade workers and Aboriginal clients and immigrants. The Confirmed Job program provides essential work-related items to help clients remain in their jobs. MHR provides employment services for persons with disabilities, including tax exemptions, planning services and Therapeutic Volunteer Services to enable the disabled to gain work experience.

Health Benefits

Residents of British Columbia are insured under the Medical Services Plan (MSP), which requires payment of a premium. Premium assistance (ranging from 20 to 100 percent) is available for low-income residents not receiving Income Assistance. In addition, the BC Fair PharmCare program—which combined BC's universal medical plan and seniors plan into one program in May 2003—subsidizes prescription drugs and designates medical supplies for low and moderate income MSP members. A dental program also provides basic dental coverage over two years "to clients who are most in need and least likely to become financially independent."[5]

Dietary supplements assistance is available on a short-term basis where medically specified. A monthly nutritional supplement program, medical transportation program and so-called "enhanced health assistance" are available to former IAP clients and their children. In addition to MSP and PharmCare, eligible clients (employed single or two-parent families) have access to certain medical equipment, supplies and non-extended dental benefits.

MHR also offers several health benefits subprograms for IAP clients. They are: Monthly Natal Supplement ($45.00 per month to pregnant women); Optical Program for persons aged 19–64; and the Supplementary Health Care Benefits program (which includes chiropractic, massage therapy, naturopathy, physical therapy and non-surgical podiatry). MHR also provides Therapeutic Volunteer Supplements program designed for clients facing multiple barriers to employment—such as physical or mental disabilities—on income support to volunteer as a pathway towards employability. Under the Healthy Kids program, children qualify for coverage of dental and vision care if their family is receiving full or partial MSP premium assistance.

Social Housing

BC Housing is a provincial crown agency that develops, manages and administers subsidized housing. It administers 33,200 units of social housing managed by non-profit societies and cooperatives, and provides annual operating subsidies for them. BC Housing also manages about 7,800 public housing units. The development of public housing has been replaced by programs that provide financial, administrative and technical support to community groups and agencies for the provision of social housing. The Provincial Housing Program helps fund the development of new non-profit and co-operative subsidized housing for frail seniors, people at risk of homelessness, people with disabilities and low-income families. As of February 2005, over 3,054 of 3,400 units of subsidized housing have been completed.[6] Independent Living BC is a federal-provincial initiative for the creation of affordable senior housing through partnerships with the private sector.

Other B.C. social housing programs include Independent Living BC (ILBC) aimed at seniors and persons with disabilities; Provincial Homelessness Initiative (PHI), which includes lowered shelter rates for employed families; and the Community Partnership Initiatives (CPI), which provides grants to community partners constructing affordable housing. Rental assistance is available to seniors in the Shelter Aid for Elderly Renters (SAFER) and the Independent Living BC programs.

Child Care

Under the auspices of the Ministry of Children and Family Development, B.C. provides one-time funding for projects that increase accessibility to child care programs in multicultural and Aboriginal communities. Low-income families are eligible for subsidies ranging from partial to full dependent on number of children and income through the Child Care Subsidy program. The Supported Child Care program supports the provision of community services to children with special needs between the ages birth to 12 in integrated care settings. Special needs youths ages 13–18 may also be eligible for supported child care services. Under the Child in the Home of a Relative Program, earning exemptions are available to family members caring for children with disabilities. Low-income families with special needs children and youths may also access the At Home Respite program; Family Support Services; child and youth care workers; Residential Services program; Nursing Support Services; and Early Intensive Behavioural Intervention programs. Child care benefits available to low-income families include a child care subsidy and subsidized housing.

Alberta

Income Security

Under the umbrella of the "Alberta Works Program," Alberta provides Income Support Benefit Services (formally, Supports for Independence) "to individuals and families who do not have resources to meet their basic needs...."[7] The underlying objective of Income Support Benefit Services (ISBS) is to provide a range of programs and supports in both cash and kind that encourage low-income families to stay in the work force and to become fully independent. The philosophy underpinning ISBS is to offer a "hand-up," not a "hand-out." In this manner, the government of Alberta claims to be moving towards lowering the so-called "welfare wall." That is, by providing extended benefits to low-income families, working parents will not find themselves "worse off in low paying jobs as compared with being on welfare."[8]

Eligibility for ISBS is based on criteria that amount to means-tested standards. Those who qualify are generally categorized as either "not expected to work," "expected to work" or "learners." Services and benefits vary by "client type," that is, by which category the person is initially assessed. Financial benefits (cash payments) are divided into three levels:

1. Core income support payments, which include shelter, food, clothing, household supplies, personal needs, transportation, and telephone;
2. Supplementary income support payments, which include AADAC allowance, children's school allowance, damage deposit, babysitting, natal allowance, and emergency allowances to cover unforeseeable circumstances between benefit periods; and
3. Any other income support payments, which include emergency assistance for utility disconnection, one-time emergency relief for farmers to assist with items essential to health care and well-being, as well as one-time financial help for persons escaping family violence.

Financial benefits, as well as medical benefits, are also provided for adults with severe and permanent disabilities under the Assured Income for the Severely Handicapped (AISH). The Income Support program for low-income widows and widowers between the ages of 55 and 64—formerly known as Widows' Pension—was replaced in March 2006 with a new income support program. The Alberta Seniors Benefit program provides a cash benefit as well as medical subsidies to eligible senior citizens. A one-time "lump sum" cash payment for low-income seniors experiencing unusual financial difficulties is also available through the Special Needs Assistance for Seniors program. This is a "last resort" program that is income tested.[9]

Other financial benefits provided at the provincial level include the Alberta Family Employment Tax Credit, which is a non-taxable financial benefit paid to low income, working families that have dependent children. The program is fully funded by the province and administered by the Canada Revenue Agency. Federal commitments to low-income families in Alberta include Old Age Security/Guaranteed Income Supplement, Canada Pension Plan, Employment Insurance, Canada Child Tax Benefit (CCTB) and GST credit. The National Child Benefit (NCB) is a joint initiative of federal, provincial and territorial governments.

Benefits in "kind" for those who are eligible for Income Support include an number of subprograms. Employment and Training Services provide skills development and training, labor market information, and access to computers, fax machines, and telephones for work search purposes. Child Support Services include individual access to a child support worker who provides assistance with court orders and Maintenance Enforcement Programs.

Health Benefits

Residents of Alberta pay a health care insurance premium to receive access to hospital and health services deemed medically necessary under the plan. However, if an Alberta resident is eligible for Income Support, the resident and his or her dependents will receive premium-free health insurance coverage, coverage for prescription drugs (as defined on either the Drug Benefit List or the Alberta Human Resources and Employment Drug Benefit List), eye and dental care, essential diabetic supplies, and emergency ambulance services. However, children in low-income families not on Income Support may be eligible for comparable coverage under the Alberta Child Health Benefit (ACHB) program, introduced in 1998 under the re-investment terms of the NCB. Coverage includes dental care, eyeglasses, prescription drugs, ambulance services, and basic diabetic supplies. Other basic medical supplies and equipment costs for children as well as low-income adults, such as wheelchairs and hearing aids, are provided by the Alberta Aids to Daily Living Program.

Alberta provides a number of other health benefits subprograms. Alberta Adult Health Benefit provides premium assistance, dental, optical and diabetic supplies and services as well as emergency ambulance services. Alberta Aids to Daily Living is a program administered by Alberta Health and Wellness and supplies medical equipment to those who have a chronic illness or who may be terminally ill and is primarily a cost-share program. The Alberta Health Care Insurance Plan Premiums program, includes the Premium Subsidy Program (through which monthly premiums are

65

lowered dependent upon taxable family income), and the Waiver of Premium program (through which insurance premiums may be eliminated for up to six months and is based on family income for three months prior to application). The Coverage for Seniors Plan helps senior citizens age 65 and over with costs of prescription drugs. For diabetics who have a low income, the Alberta Monitoring for Health program provides assistance for managing diet needs as well as oral medications and insulin therapy. The AISH program also provides prescription drugs, eyeglasses, eye exams, dental work, emergency ambulance services and essential diabetic supplies. Persons with Developmental Disabilities, Alberta Brain Injury Initiative, Family Support for Children with Disabilities and the Home Adaptation program all provide focus-specific services and benefits such as counselling, costs for disability-related clothing and footwear, aides, equipment and supplies. These programs aim to reduce a significant barrier to employment attachment.

Social Housing

Alberta maintains a number of subsidy programs for low-income families, as well as programs targeting low-income senior citizens, shelters for the homeless, and those fleeing family violence. The Community Housing Program provides subsidized rental housing for low-income families, senior citizens, and others in need. The Rent Supplement Program provides rent subsidies to private landlords to provide low-income households in need with suitable accommodations. Two programs for which capital funding is no longer available are the Private Non-Profit Housing Program, which allows private non-profit organizations to own social housing projects, and the Rural and Native Housing Program, which provides rental accommodation to low-income families in rural communities. Under the latter program, assistance was provided for the low-income household's monthly rental.

Alberta Seniors and Community Supports Program also offers a Housing Registry that provides grants to eight housing registries. These registries aim to find housing for households in trouble and difficult to house persons, and at the same time collect information on the nature of household problems at the heart of displacement. Two registries are designated for seniors; six are for Family and Special Purpose Housing. The Special Purpose Housing Program provides mortgage subsidy to non-profit organizations for financing to enable the development of housing for special needs tenants—such as emergency or transitional residences—as well as facilities for people with physical, mental or behavioural challenges and for those victims of family violence, ex-convicts and hard-to-house.

Social housing that focuses on low-income seniors is divided into six subprograms. Seniors Lodge Program for functionally independent senior citizens, includes a sitting room, housekeeping and recreational services. Cottage Program, formerly known as the Seniors Self-Contained Housing Program for functionally independent seniors, provides apartment-style accommodation, (however, no additional services such as housekeeping and food are supplied). Unique Homes Program offers low-income seniors supportive housing in lodge-type housing. These units are owned and/or managed by not-for-profit organizations. Senior's Housing Registry Program maintains lists of senior's apartments and lodges, assists in locating private seniors accommodation, and documents household problems. Finally, the Seniors Supportive Housing Incentive Program, initiated in 2000, funds housing projects for low and modest-income senior citizens. Capital funding is no longer available for the Healthy Aging Partnership Initiative Program.

Social housing for Alberta's homeless, under the auspices of Alberta's Community Development "Moving Forward" initiative, is a program that provides a continuum of housing facilities and support services, such as emergency shelters and transitional housing. Each community is responsible for developing and implementing a "continuum of housing" plan. Community initiatives are reviewed by provincial and federal governments. There are also numerous community initiatives providing shelters that target women leaving household violence. The aim of Alberta's social housing programs is to provide low-income singles, families, seniors and special needs persons with accommodation that is affordable, safe and stable.

Child Care

National Child Care Benefits (NCB) reinvestment funds have been used to expand several programs targeting child care in —including the province's daycare subsidy program—and to raise the net income qualification levels for the child care subsidy. The objective of provincial (and territorial and First Nations) NCB re-investments was to reduce social assistance payments to families with children, in turn savings accrued would be "redirected" into programs benefiting children of low-income families. In essence, the goal of NCB re-investments was to help low-income working parents remain in the labour market. Programs that have been targeted for expansion include:

1. Protection of Children Involved in Prostitution program provides services to help children disengage from prostitution and allows for detaining child prostitutes for up to five days in a secured facility where he or she receives emergency care and an assessment;

2. Youths in transition from the Child Welfare program to Independent living; and

3. Alberta's Child Care Subsidy Program provides financial assistance, based on family income and number of children as well as hours of childcare required on a monthly basis for children aged 0–7 in approved programs for working parents, parents enroled in an educational program, or special needs child or parent.

Saskatchewan

Income Security

68

Saskatchewan provides a basic "program of last resort for families and individuals who, for various reasons, including disability, illness, low income or unemployment, cannot meet their basic living costs."[10] Eligibility is based on a needs test. In addition to financial assistance for basic needs, the program provides supplementary health coverage, which provides coverage for prescription drugs, dental and optical services, as well as other medically required services. For low income clients enrolled in basic education and bridging programs, the Provincial Training Allowance (PTA) provides financial assistance with the cost of living while they maintain enrollment in educational programs approved for PTA funding. Supplementary health coverage is provided for PTA recipients and their families.

In addition, there are several programs to supplement low income. For low-income families with dependent children, the Saskatchewan Employment Supplement (SES) provides a monthly supplement to income earned from wages, self-employment and child/spousal maintenance payments. In addition to the financial benefit, SES recipients also receive supplementary health coverage through the Family Health Benefits program. The Saskatchewan Child Benefit is integrated with the Canadian Child Tax Benefit to provide financial assistance to lower income families with dependent children. The program is fully funded by the province and administered by Canada Revenue Agency. The Saskatchewan Income Plan provides financial assistance for low-income senior residents.

The underlying objective of Saskatchewan's income support program is to move clients from "dependence on social assistance to the work force"[11] and to help working individuals and families remain in the labour market. In order to "build independence" employables on assistance are expected to look for work, or take training or educational upgrading. Income assistance subprograms providing allowances to low-income working persons include a Shelter Allowance; Utility Allowance; Northern Food Allowance; and a Special Needs Allowance to assist disabled, low-income persons to enter and remain in the work force. This allowance also provides limited financial support for parents waiting for the Child Benefit. Career and Employment Counselling Services are provided to all clients along with a Jobs First and Transitional Employment allowance that seeks to help people remain in the work force.

Health Benefits

Saskatchewan's health insurance plan covers all medically necessary services provided by physicians; occupational and physiotherapy services; screening (mammography, HIV, STD) and immunization services; optometric services for children under 18 years of age; drug and alcohol abuse treatment; and mental health services. In addition to the basic coverage provided to all provincial residents under the health insurance plan, the Family Health Benefits program provides supplementary health coverage for dental, optical, emergency ambulatory and chiropractic services to families eligible for the Saskatchewan Child Benefit and the Saskatchewan Employment Supplement. The Supplementary Health Program provides coverage for medically required drugs, supplies, appliances and services for residents in need. Eligibility is determined by Saskatchewan Social Services. The Saskatchewan Aids to Independent Living (SAIL) program provides coverage for services and special needs equipment required by people with long-term disabilities or illnesses that impair their ability to function. Universal coverage for prescription medication is provided by the Saskatchewan Drug Plan. Two programs that are based on need extend drug benefits: the Emergency Prescription Drug Assistance program temporarily covers the full cost of prescription medication; the Special Support Program provides full coverage for households whose drug costs are high in relation to their income.

Social Housing

The Saskatchewan Housing Corporation (SHC) provides access to affordable housing for low- and moderate-income families, seniors, and the disabled through the development, delivery and administration of a variety of housing programs. The programs include rent subsidy programs; grants to municipalities, non-profit organizations and co-operatives to assist development of affordable housing; and repair, conversion and rehabilitation programs that offer assistance. SHC owns about 18,400 units of the 30,400 social housing units, which are owned by local housing authorities, non-profit organizations, housing co-operatives and private landlords.

In 2004–2005 the Home First program was introduced. This program expects to build 2,000 new low-income housing units by 2008, provide a housing supplement for disabled and invest $200 million in approximately

17,000 low-income households.[12] Transition Houses provide emergency shelter for women and children.

Child Care

Saskatchewan licenses and monitors child care facilities. It provides child care subsidies for low-income families, and grant funding for the expansion of daycare spaces. Subsidies may also be provided for alternative daycare—in-home licensed and non-profit centres—for low-income working families. As well, funding is available for special needs children in an integrated setting. The Child Nutrition and Development program and the Kids First program target high risk children in order to help them get a "better start" in life. The Teen and Young Parent program provides counselling services and skills training to support low-income teens.

Manitoba

Income Security

The shift from welfare state to residual state in federal social policy was reflected in the drop in welfare rolls in Manitoba from 85,200 in 1995 to 59,900 in 2003, a decline of 29.7 percent.[13] In the area of income security, Manitoba has an Employment and Income Assistance program (EIA), a "program of last resort for people who need help to meet basic personal and family needs."[14] Eligibility is based on a needs test that compares the total financial resources of a household to the total cost of basic necessities such as food, clothing and shelter. The underlying objective of EIA is to help employables find work and/or remain in the work force. The program provides a continuum of financial benefits for basic needs (food, clothing, and shelter) based on geography (northern, rural or urban) and status (single persons with/without children, couples with/without children and two-parent families).

EIA includes the following subprograms: Assistance for Special Needs Costs; Newborn Assistance Program; Major Appliances and Essential Household Furnishings program; Assistance for Beds and Bedding program; Moving Costs program, specifically for job training or to lower living costs; School Supplies program for children grades Kindergarten to 12 of low-income families; Employment Benefits for Persons with Disabilities, for working disabled to purchase work related items such as clothing, transportation and unexpected medical costs and subsidized child care; and the Self-Employment program, designed to assist with developing business plans and training. EIA also provides assistance to clients for obtaining child support and maintenance. The philosophy underpinning

EIA programs is called "work expectation." That is, unless a person is confronted with special needs or circumstances, all recipients of EIA are expected to actively search for work and remain in the work force once there. Within this framework EIA offers a Building Independence initiative designed as a resource to "link training and employment for income assistance participants with other government departments."[15]

In addition to financial benefits to cover basic needs, the program provides health benefits that include subsidies for prescription drugs, dental care, eyeglasses and hearing aids, and chiropractic services. Individuals who do not need assistance with basic living costs may apply for financial assistance to pay for their health care. The Child Related Income Support Program (CRISP) provides financial assistance to low-income families not receiving EIA. Eligibility is based on receipt of the Canada Child Tax Benefit and means.

Health Benefits

Manitoba residents are insured under the Manitoba Health Services Insurance Plan. The plan covers standard medical services, as well as optometrist services for children and seniors, chiropractor services (up to a maximum of 12 visits per year), medical assessments, hearing aids, wheelchairs (and repairs), as well as certain medical supplies and equipment and some dental surgeon services. In addition, the Healthy Child Manitoba program has initiated a number of subprograms targeted at children and youth at risk in terms of health outcomes: Healthy Baby assists low-income pregnant women to meet their extra nutritional needs and provides community-based support services; BabyFirst provides a three-year home visiting program for newborns and their families; STOP FAS is a three-year mentoring program for women at risk of having a child with fetal alcohol syndrome (FAS) or fetal alcohol effects. Manitoba has partnered with the governments of British Columbia, Alberta, Saskatchewan, Nunavut, the Northwest Territories and the Yukon to raise awareness of FAS.

Manitoba provides access to affordable housing for families, seniors and single people living on low and moderate incomes. The Manitoba Housing Authority manages public housing units. In addition, there is a range of programs that provides subsidies for private housing units, such as the sponsor-managed public housing program, private non-profit program, rent supplement program, rural and native housing, and urban native non-profit housing program.[16] The rent supplement programs for families and for seniors illustrate the nature of these programs. The Shelter Allowances for Family Renters (SAFFR) program provides financial assistance for rent subsidies to low income families who rent accommodations in the private market. The Shelter Allowances for Elderly Renters (SAFER) program provides rental housing subsidies to low-income seniors. In addition, the Residential Rehabilitation Assistance program (RRAP) is a federal-provincial cost-shared program that provides financial assistance to eligible homeowners and landlords of rental units. This assistance is targeted at low-income tenants for the rehabilitation of existing substandard housing that requires major repairs, or for alterations required to make a unit accessible and comfortable for persons living with disabilities. The Home Adaptations for Seniors' Independence (HASI) program provides financial assistance for home adaptation to maintain low-income seniors in the home.

72

Child Care

Manitoba's Child Care program offers partial subsidies for low-income parents if they are working, actively looking for work or are enrolled in an educational or job training program. Other child care subprograms for EIA recipients include Children's Special Services which consists of counselling, respite care, therapy, supplies and equipment, transportation and child development; Child Day Care for Children with Disabilities program offers support for inclusion in daycare programs for disabled children; Children in Care with Disabilities program; and a school supplies program for children under age of 18. Manitoba Child Care program also licenses and monitors child care centres and homes. It provides grants and program assistance to eligible facilities and works to place children with disabilities in appropriate facilities. Child care subsidies are provided for low-income families.

Ontario

Income Security

Two basic income assistance programs provide financial assistance. The Ontario Works program provides financial assistance "only when all other financial resources have been exhausted."[17] Eligibility is based on means-tested criteria and agreement to participate in employment assistance activities. In addition to financial benefits for basic needs—food, clothing and shelter—the program provides coverage for prescription drugs. The underlying objective of the Ontario Works program is to encourage clients to achieve self-sufficiency through entering and remaining in the work force. Accordingly, an employment assistance program provides clients with job search related services, community volunteer opportunities and work preparation skills. Addiction treatment and literacy training is also available as part of the Employment Assistance program.

The Ontario Disability Support Program provides financial assistance and employment supports to low-income adults with disabilities—those with a substantial physical or mental impairment that is continuous or recurrent and is expected to last one year or more. In addition to the two social allowance programs, Ontario has two demogrant programs for low and moderate income households: the Ontario Child Care Supplement for Working Families is a tax-free monthly payment to low and moderate-income households with children under age seven; the Ontario Guaranteed Annual Income System ensures a guaranteed minimum income to senior citizens. The Workplace Child Care Tax Credit supports businesses that invest in building or renovating licensed child care facilities for children of working parents.

73

Health Benefits

Ontario residents are eligible for coverage of hospital and physician services under the Ontario Health Insurance Plan (OHIP). Services provided by podiatrists, chiropractors and osteopaths are partially covered; physiotherapy services are provided in approved facilities; dental surgery in hospitals; and optometry services biannually. In addition, the Ontario Drug Benefit Program covers most of the cost of prescription drugs for the following categories of residents: seniors; residents in long-term care facilities, or homes for special care; and people receiving professional services under the home care program. The Trillium Drug Program provides a subsidy for specified prescription drugs for people who have high drug costs in relation to their income.

The Ontario Disability Support program provides financial benefits and prescription drug coverage as well as limited dental and optical benefits to persons with disabilities between the ages of 18 and 64. Benefits include hearing aids, assistive devices and a small school allowance for dependent children.

Social Housing

The province got out of the business of social housing in 2000 by devolving the administration of social housing into the municipalities.[18] By 2002, administration of the province's approximately 84,000 public housing units had been transferred from the Ontario Housing Authority to Local Housing Authorities.[19] In its place, in May 2002 the province initiated the Affordable Housing Program as a federal-provincial joint initiative to stimulate construction of affordable housing. Under the program, the Community Rental Housing Program began as a pilot project to stimulate construction of affordable housing for the low-income tenant market; the

Remote Program to rehabilitate, renovate or replace substandard housing in the northern geographic area also commenced. In addition, the Ontario Home Ownership Savings Plan is a savings plan program and refundable tax credit to lower-income individuals to save towards the purchase of a first home.

In April 2005, the federal government and the government of Ontario entered into a new agreement to cost share building 15,000 units of affordable housing between 2005 and 2009 with a special emphasis on housing for seniors. A portion of the funding is directed towards rent supplements in existing housing.

Child Care

The Ministry of Children and Youth Services licenses and monitors child care programs and agencies. It also supports fee subsidies toward the cost of licensed child care for low-income families and for parents with children with special needs. The Ontario Child Care Supplement for Working Families program provides benefits to low- and moderate-income families for in-home child care if one or both parents are working or enrolled in a training or education program. In addition, it provides wage subsidies to enhance the salaries and benefits of staff employed in licensed child care agencies and resource centres, and to home child care providers. A special needs program provides staff, equipment, supplies and services to support children with special needs in integrated child care settings. Ontario's Youth Justice Services provides rehabilitative programs aimed at high risk youths and includes therapy, education, intervention, life skills training, substance abuse and employment counselling. Particular attention is paid to cultural needs of Aboriginal youths.

Quebec

Income Security

Quebec maintains a program for last-resort financial assistance, the Employment Assistance Program. Eligibility is based on proof that "resources (cash, property, earnings, benefits and income) are equal to or less than the amounts prescribed by regulation."[20] In addition to financial assistance to cover the basic needs of adults in the household, the Employment Assistance Program provides a special housing assistance benefit for Employment Assistance recipients with at least one dependent child, and medical assistance program to cover special health needs. Emploi-Quebec provides financial assistance to Employment Assistance recipients participating in an employment assistance strategy. For employed parents, the Work Premium program—formerly Parental Wage Assistance (PWA)—provides additional financial benefits to low-income workers with at least one dependent child; child care assistance for each child attending a low-cost daycare centre; and prepayment of refundable child care expenses tax credit. There is also a family benefits program for parents with at least one dependent child that offers both financial assistance for low-income families and additional financial assistance for families with a dependent handicapped child.

Income support is also offered to workers affected by collective dismissals and to employable people between the ages of 18–24 to upgrade education, job search or participate in job training programs. Quebec Pluriel program is aimed at visible minority school drop-outs to help develop job skills and to upgrade their educations.

The underlying objective of Quebec's income support programs is to combat poverty and social exclusion. Employment and training are designated as government priorities to promote this goal. The Quebec government acknowledges that the globalization of markets will present challenges to the population's job futures. Therefore, under the rubric of "Welfare to Work," support programs aim to foster work skills and training that will ensure sustainable employment.[21]

Health Benefits

Quebec is unique in ensuring universal health and child care access to all residents. In the area of health benefits for residents, Quebec has a health insurance plan that covers physician and hospital services, certain optometric and dental services, and essential medical devices and prostheses. There is also a public drug insurance plan for Quebec residents who are not covered by a private plan. Special Benefits are available to assist with specific medical expenses, such as diabetes, colostomies and medical conditions requiring oxygen. Extended Health Benefits are available for pregnant mothers and mothers of infants.

Social Housing

Quebec administers a variety of programs to provide low and moderate-income families access to affordable and suitable housing. AccèsLogis Québec is a financial assistance program that promotes the coordination of public, private and community resources to build social and community housing for low- and moderate-income households and clients with special housing needs. The social housing program includes 65,000 units of public low-rental housing, and 8,200 units of private low-rental housing; a rent supplements program is also provided to over 12,000 low-income families and is administered by housing bureaus, cooperatives and non-profit organizations; a shelter allowance program; and an affordable housing program. A shelter allowance is provided for individuals and families on income support; persons with mental health issues or substance abuse; recent discharges from the correctional system; women fleeing household violence; and for the homeless and hard-to-house.

Child Care

Quebec ensures that child daycare services are available at minimal cost by offering subsidized daycare services for the dependent children of all residents through private for-profit daycare centres. Quebec's Maternity Allowance Program (PRALMA) pays support to pregnant women awaiting receipt of Employment Insurance premiums. A Nursing Benefit is available to breast-feeding mothers for a period of one year from the birth of the child. Expectant mothers are also eligible for a special Pregnancy Benefit. For parents of infants 0–9 months, financial assistance is available for the purchase of formula. Low-income minors may also receive financial assistance. School Expenses Benefits program helps low-income families with basic in-school expenses.

New Brunswick

Income Security

New Brunswick has a social assistance program available to "a person in need or likely to become a person in need unless assistance is provided in accordance with this Act and the regulations."[22] In addition to financial assistance to cover the costs of basic needs for the applicant and dependents—including food, clothing and shelter—the program provides health benefits that include dental, optical care and prescription drugs, and subsidized daycare; items of special need; funeral and burial assistance, and special care assistance.[23] There is also a Day Care Assistance Program available for low-income families not receiving income security.

New Brunswick's Department of Family and Community Services offers several subprograms to clients using social assistance: work preparation, education upgrading, employment training, job-search and work experience programs. The department provides grants to non-profit community volunteer agencies under the Community Volunteer Action program to assist low-income, working families and individuals with basic needs. The underlying objective of these programs is to get clients back to work. This objective is reflected in New Brunswick's philosophical framework—"set your course for work today"—underpinning services and benefits provided by the department.[24]

For low-income families with dependent children, the New Brunswick Child Tax Benefit is a non-taxable benefit. The New Brunswick Working Income Supplement is an additional benefit to low-income families with earned income. The program is fully funded by the province and administered by the Canada Revenue Agency. New Brunswick also offers several tax credit programs for low-income persons with disabilities for medical expenses as well as a Child Disability Benefit—a supplement to Canada Child Tax Benefit and Children's Special Allowance. In addition, clients may receive assistance with collecting child support and maintenance and judicial proceedings to secure child support.

77

Health Benefits

New Brunswick residents are insured under the province's Medicare program. Most medically required services provided by physicians are insured, as well as specified dental surgeries and hospital services. Low-income New Brunswick residents and those clients using income assistance programs are eligible for several health services programs: the rehabilitation program, hearing aid, vision, hyperalimentation, orthopedic, pharmaceutical, prosthetic, wheelchair and diabetic supplies programs.

Social Housing

New Brunswick maintains a commitment "to assist residents who have limited incomes in their efforts to obtain adequate, suitable and affordable accommodations."[25] To this end, the province maintains a broad-based housing program that includes public housing with 4,268 units. Under the Rural and Native Housing Program, the province owns and maintains 913 rental units for low income families. Complementing public housing programs, the Non-Profit Social Housing Program provides subsidies to non-profit organizations for social housing. In addition to this program, the Rental Supplement Program subsidizes rental accommodations for low-income families, seniors and the disabled. The Community Initiatives Program provides one-time grants to community groups and private non-profit organizations to construct or acquire and operate affordable housing projects for low-income families, seniors and persons with special needs.

There are also several federal-provincial initiatives to increase the availability of affordable housing. The Rental and Rooming house Program assists low-income rental households to upgrade existing substandard units. Similarly, the Rental Conversion Program provides financial assistance to owners to convert non-residential properties into affordable, self-contained rental accommodations for low-income households. The Shelter Enhancement Program provides financial assistance in the form of forgivable loans to sponsors of existing shelters for victims of family violence for the purpose of repairing and improving the accommodations. There are also several programs targeted at low and modest income homeowners.[26]

Child Care

New Brunswick's Excellence in Parenting Program administered by the Department of Family and Community Services in partnership with the National Child Benefit program (NCB) supports low-income families with children through the New Brunswick Child Tax Benefit and the New Brunswick working income supplement. New Brunswick also provides a "Healthy Minds" breakfast program; a Day Care Assistance program that includes partial subsidies for low-income working parents; and an Alternative Child Care Assistance program that provides financial assistance to low and modest income families using non-licensed daycare or babysitting services in order to help parents remain in the work force or in training or educational programs. New Brunswick offers financial assistance and provides a prenatal program to low-income expectant mothers and an Unmarried Parents Service for pregnant women and birth fathers who may be considering adoption. New Brunswick's Intensive Support program targets youths at risk and offers several subprograms including Emergency Social Services, Child Victims of Abuse, Intervention, Educational Tutoring, Employment and Life Skills programs as well as a Youth Treatment program.

Newfoundland and Labrador

Income Security

Newfoundland's Income Support Program provides financial assistance for persons in need. Eligibility is based on consideration of "the needs of the individual or family…compared with all the resources of the applicant and the applicant's family."[27] Income Support Benefits program encompasses both basic and non-basic financial assistance. Basic benefits include food, clothing, shelter and some household supplies. Non-basic benefits include a housekeeper's allowance, child benefit, emergency services, private child care and burial expenses. Clients are also eligible for a health care card— which covers approved prescription drugs, dispensing fees and limited dental coverage—some medical equipment and school supplies.

The underlying objective of Newfoundland and Labrador income support program is "working towards employment," that is, getting recipients into the labour force and keeping them there. Clients may also be eligible for several income support subprograms such as: Newfound Jobs and Earning Supplements (both programs provide financial assistance with work-related items such as transportation and clothing); Extensive Employment; Training Support; and Job Search programs. In addition, the Newfoundland and Labrador Child Benefit (NLCB) is a family allowance program designed to help low-income families with the cost of raising children. It provides a tax-free monthly benefit that is combined with the Canada Child Tax Benefit into a single monthly payment. The child benefit program is fully funded by the province.

Health Benefits

The province's Medical Care Plan provides covers the cost of physician services for all provincial residents. Hospital services are covered under the Newfoundland Hospital Insurance Plan. In Newfoundland and Labrador's "Partnering for Health" initiative (2001) multiple levels of government, in tandem with community services and the private sector, have linked to co-ordinate and provide low-income individuals and families with health benefits programs such as the Healthy Baby Club, Support Trusts for Disabled Persons and the Stepping into the Future program, which focuses on children and youths with mental health, pregnancy and literacy issues. In addition, there are a number of health benefit programs targeted at low-income households. The Newfoundland and Labrador Prescription Drug Program subsidizes the cost of prescription medicine for low-income seniors and persons with designated special medication needs. In addition, the Mother Baby Nutrition Supplement provides $45 per month to low-income pregnant women and families with children less than one year of age.

Social Housing

The housing arm of the provincial government is the Newfoundland and Labrador Housing Corporation (NLHC) which was incorporated in 1967 to provide suitable and affordable housing for low-income families. NLHC operates three programs: the Provincial Home Repair Program (PHRP); Rental Housing Program; and the Rent Supplement Program. PHRP provides grants and repayable loans to eligible low-income homeowners who require essential repairs, improvements or modifications to their home. The Rental Housing Program rents housing to low-income families and others in need—those who have to pay more than 30 percent of their income for adequate housing—and works with groups that agree to provide housing for low-income households. The Rent Supplement Program subsidizes rent in the private rental accommodations sector for low-income households that pay more than 30 percent of their total household income towards the cost of rent and heat.[28]

Child Care

Newfoundland and Labrador offer a child care services subsidy to low-income working families and an Early Childhood Development program, which includes financial assistance and information services for pregnant women, a baby food allowance, pre-kindergarten literacy programs, and intervention programs for children with autism. Under the Stepping into the Future program, families with children experiencing developmental delays and behavioural problems can access consultation and assessment services. Grants are also available under the Family Home Child Care program to purchase equipment and to increase availability of services to low-income families. In addition, the Mother Baby Nutrition Supplement provides $45 per month to low-income pregnant women and families with children less than one year of age.

Nova Scotia

Income Security

Nova Scotia's Employment Support and Income Assistance Program (ESIA) provides "for the assistance of persons in need and, in particular, to facilitate their movement toward independence and self-sufficiency."[29] Eligibility is based on the principle of need, which the ESIA Manual states "must be paramount in determining eligibility for income assistance."[30] Eligibility criteria include income, expenses and efforts to obtain employment. In addition to financial assistance for basic needs—food, clothing, and shelter—ESIA benefits include assistance to pay for prescription drugs, limited dental and optic care; transportation and child care for the purpose of employment; health and safety; and expenses prescribed for applicable special needs, such as medical needs.

The underlying objective of Nova Scotia's income security program is to promote self-sufficiency primarily through encouraging clients to enter and remain in the work force. Accordingly, Nova Scotia offers several subprograms to clients or recent leavers of income support: Employment Support Services offers career planning, counselling, academic upgrading, training programs, volunteer initiatives and access to equipment for job search purposes; a School Supplies program for families with children ages

5–18; and a Special Needs program to assist with the unique needs that a low-income person requires to find work or remain employed, which includes transportation, child care, special diets, emergency shelter, rental deposits and some furniture. Allowances for children are excluded from ESIA; rather, they are covered by an income support program for all low-income families with children, the Nova Scotia Child Benefit. Benefits from this program are combined with the federal Canada Child Tax Benefit into a single, non-taxable monthly payment. The program is fully funded by the province.

Health Benefits

The Nova Scotia Health Insurance Plan insures residents with coverage for medically required hospital, medical, dental and optometric services. In addition, the province's Pharmacare program provides assistance to seniors to help pay for prescription drugs, and to low-income cancer patients and multiple sclerosis patients to help pay for treatment drugs. An extended Pharmacare program offers limited financial assistance to low-income working families who have left income assistance and need help with drug costs. Nova Scotia's program "Services for Persons with Disabilities" provides both residential and day programs, as well as unlicensed and licensed homes, for care and support of disabled persons. There are also centres that provide training for disabled persons to help them find employment.

Social Housing

The Housing Services Division of the Department of Community Services administers a number of grant and loan programs funded through a federal-provincial initiative that are designed to help low to moderate income households maintain or acquire adequate and affordable accommodations. The Provincial Housing Emergency Repair Program provides assistance to low-income households to carry out emergency repairs on their homes. The Emergency Repair Program assists low-income homeowners in rural areas to make emergency repairs. The Senior Citizens Assistance Program (SCAP) and Home Adaptations for Seniors Independence (HASI) provide grants to eligible homeowners and landlords to carry out necessary repairs and adaptations for seniors. The Access-A-Home Program provides grants to households who must adapt their homes for wheelchair use.

In addition to the grant programs, there are several loan programs. The Small Loans Assistance Program provides low-interest loans to moderate-income households for home improvements. The Parent Apartment

Program provides low-interest loans for additions or renovations to a single family dwelling to accommodate a senior apartment. The Family Modest Housing Program provides funds for lower and middle-income families to build or buy modest housing. Nova Scotia housing authorities owns 12,000 rental supplement units and co-operative housing available to low-income families and seniors.

Child Care

The Department of Community Services licenses and monitors child care programs in Nova Scotia. It also provides child care subsidies for parents who need child care when working or while attending training programs. In addition, it provides grants to child development centres to enable preschool-aged children from disadvantaged families and children-at-risk to participate in head-start or enrichment programs. Funding is also provided to child care centres to provide appropriate program-ming for young children with special needs. In addition, Early Childhood Development services offer a supported child care program for special needs children, which includes the services of therapists, early interven-tionists and educators as well as developmental professionals.

Prince Edward Island

Income Security

The province's Financial Assistance Program (FAS) provides financial assis-tance for "the basic necessities of living to those who for physical, mental, social or other reasons are unable to provide for their own basic needs."[31] Basic needs include shelter, food, and clothing, assistance with utility bills, household supplies, a pre-natal food allowance, local transportation and a Healthy Child allowance. Financial assistance is also available for specified special needs items such as transportation to job training sites, employment relocation, some medical transportation and supplies, as well as special clothing, respite and some housekeeping needs. Special Needs program will cover limited burial costs, dental, optical and hearing aids. Eligibility is based on a needs assessment. In addition to financial assis-tance, health benefits include coverage for prescription drugs, essential optical and dental care.

Health Benefits

Physician and hospital services are insured for all provincial residents under Prince Edward Islands' Hospital and Medical Services Plans. The Family Health Benefit Program subsidizes the cost of prescription medications for low-income families with children and seniors; the Seniors Drug Cost Assistance Plan subsidizes the cost of prescription and some non-prescription medications for senior residents. Two programs provide assistance with the high cost of medications related to two chronic illnesses: the Diabetes Control Program and the Multiple Sclerosis Program. Prince Edward Island's Children-in-Care program covers the cost of all medications required by children under the age of 18 who are wards of the province. There are several drug assistance programs provided by the Provincial Pharmacy program, for cystic fibrosis, eprex, immunizations, meningitis, and all STD's and tuberculosis programs.

Social Housing

There are two major components to the province's Social Housing Program. The Seniors Housing Program provides low and moderate income seniors over the age of 60 with accommodations (rent is calculated at 30 percent of income). The Family Housing Program provides rental housing to low and moderate income families (rent is calculated at 25 percent of income).

Child Care

The PEI Child Care Facilities board is responsible for licensing and monitoring child care and early childhood programs. The Child Care Subsidy Program subsidizes child care fees for early childhood programs. The amount of a subsidy depends on family income.

5

Social Policy Reform and the Normalization of Child Poverty

I initiated this review of Canadian social policy in an effort to understand the state of children's welfare in the Canadian welfare state. What I have discovered is that the welfare of poor children is a casualty of the ideological war on the welfare state launched in the liberal right-wing's counter-offensive[1] against the liberal left-wing's war on poverty. The purpose of this chapter is to survey the pathway from entitlement to charity through the looking glass of reform.

Social Policy Reform

Examining the problem of child poverty in Canada from an epistemological perspective, Chapter One addressed the value-laden character of facts on several dimensions—ideological, methodological and evaluative. As the examination revealed, facts serve to frame the object of discussion in a discourse within a contextual field of inferred representations derived from an ideological model of the good society. For example, in welfare state discourse facts about child poverty were framed in the contextual field of the just society; in contrast, in neo-conservative discourse they are framed in the contextual field of the competitive society. While facts serve to frame a discourse by embedding operant conditions in an idealized context, verbs serve to spin the discourse ideologically.

The verb reform is a good example of the spin function. It has dimensions of both reference and inference. As an act, reform refers to an effort "to change into an improved form or condition;" as an inference, it infers that the object of change is "defective, vicious, corrupt, or depraved."[2] What this example reflects about the concept of reform is that it not only infers a problem, it also confers a moral representation of the nature of the problem, and a prescription for its resolution. As it relates to social policy, the dimension of moral inference drives ideological spin. The moral representation function is reflected across the liberal ideological spectrum from right to left in their different core values about the nature of welfare benefits (Table 2–1), which legitimate the act of giving in terms of either volunteerism, humanitarianism or egalitarianism. Similarly, public welfare is morally justified in terms of the character of the poor as deserving/undeserving, as victims of socio-economic disadvantage or as citizens with rights to a basic standard of living.

Definitions tend to be ideologically contested issues in the realm of politics, and different definitions of social policy reform have marked watersheds of transition in Canadian social policy history. As discussed in Chapter Two, in the aftermath of the Great Depression, throughout Western Europe and North America the social policy reform agenda promoted by ethical liberalism promised to make capitalism more humane. The object of reform—capitalism—was deemed flawed by unfettered free market competition and the existence of poverty represented the moral manifestation of the flaw. The Canadian welfare state was initiated under this umbrella with two very modest income security programs: Unemployment Insurance in 1940 and Family Allowance in 1944. As reflected in Chapter Two, poverty amelioration played a central role in the Canadian welfare state's development and expansion. In fact, over the life of the welfare state era, 1943–73, the poverty driven spin of social policy development moved (decidedly, if grudgingly) from right of centre to left of centre on the spectrum of liberal ideology (Table 1–1), culminating in the 1973 Social Security Review with a proposal for a guaranteed annual income, a policy promoted by the left and contested by the right from the beginning.

In contrast to the welfare state era's social policy reform agenda for making capitalism more humane, the residual state's social policy agenda is defined in terms of making capitalism more efficient. The object of social policy reform is the welfare state, not capitalism. The moral representation of the welfare state as "defective, vicious, corrupt, or depraved" imbues the public discourse of liberal individualism, in effect vilifying both the state and welfare as impediments to the inherent systemic efficiency of the unfettered free market. Seen through this ideological lens, the existence of poverty—and therefore, the poor—are an artifact of inefficiency, moral slothfulness and a culture of dependency nurtured under the welfare state. As reflected in Chapter Three, the social policy agenda in the residual state is targeted at promoting personal responsibility for welfare through private enterprise and industry. Thus, the transition from the welfare state to the residual state represented a fundamental change in the state's role in the welfare of citizens. The Social Union Framework Agreement (SUFA) replaced the welfare state's framework of social entitlement, promoted through income security and Canada Assistance Plan (CAP) programs, with the residual state's framework of provincial capacity, promoted through equalization. Moreover, with the launching of the Voluntary Sector Initiative (VSI), voluntarism replaced the public social safety net advanced by the welfare state.

Normalization of Child Poverty

The 1989 House of Commons' resolution to eliminate child poverty by 2000 received unanimous support in Parliament across the liberal ideological spectrum—that is, on the left, New Democratic Party, led by Ed Broadbent, with his vision of social democracy; on the right, Progressive Conservative Party, led by Brian Mulroney, with his vision of economic competitiveness; and in the centre, the Liberal Party, led by John Turner, with no particular vision but political survival (especially in the context of the party's poor performance in the 1988 election). However, as reflected in Chapter Three, Parliamentary unanimity on the resolution masked very different ideological perspectives on the nature and scope of child poverty. On the one hand, the resolution reflected that there was a broad national consensus that child poverty was a significant social problem, and something could and should be done about it; on the other hand, in the political context of Parliament in 1989, it marked the passing of the banner for action—of who should do something—from the state to civil society. The transition from entitlement to charity ensued as the Canadian social safety net was dismantled in the name of reform.

Chapter One examined the role of state discourse in reforming (ideologically spinning) the terms of reference or policy principles for public action on the issue of child poverty. In effect, the nature of the problem was redefined from child poverty to child development, and from structural inequality to social vulnerability. The twentieth century narrative of state discourse on child poverty concluded as a social problem and poverty as a structural problem. From this perspective, the normalization of child poverty relates to the process of recasting the terms of reference or contextual field in which facts about child poverty are interpreted—recasting the context from just society to competitive society. The contrast between welfare state and residual state social programs examined in Chapters Two and Three reveal the relationship between the reform of policy principles and the changing course of action in federal social policy. As reflected in Chapter Two, the Canadian welfare state was founded on the principle of social entitlement. From its modest beginnings with the 1940 Unemployment Insurance Act, federal social safety net development was driven by the logic of entitlement to increase the scope of coverage. This expansion dynamic culminated with proposals for a guaranteed annual income by 1973. The 1989 House of Commons resolution to end child poverty by 2000 reverberated with the welfare state's logic of entitlement, and appealed to both the liberal left's agenda for public provision of basic needs and the liberal centre's agenda for public provision for the deserving poor (Table 2–1).

But the 1989 resolution was the last hurrah for the welfare state, as the liberal right had rewritten the policy blueprint and seized the opportunity afforded by the resolution to initiate reform of the social safety net, as discussed in Chapter Three. Dismantling of the remaining vestiges of the welfare state social policy framework ensued, and a residual policy framework was put in place in 1999 with SUFA—a social policy framework more consistent with the constitutional fundamentalism of classical federalism than with the overlapping jurisdictions and divided authority of modern federalism discussed in Chapter Two. SUFA prescribed the residual framework on two dimensions. First, it formalized the transfer of the social policy architect role from federal to provincial jurisdiction, subordinating federal spending power in the social policy area to provincial jurisdiction. Second, it limited the scope of state responsibility for the social welfare of citizens to the deserving poor—children and the disabled. As a framework for intergovernmental relations in the provision of social programs, CAP's conditional grants for provincial social services based on a program's conformity with a national standard of eligibility for public welfare benefits were replaced with SUFA's unconditional funding formula based on equalization of provincial capacity in program development. Under the SUFA framework, a plethora of social programs emerged to provide labour force attachment related rehabilitation services to poor households, as reviewed in Chapter Four. With the launching of VSI in 2000 to mobilize private sector voluntary social services, the residual model of welfare was complete.

Thus, the concept of normalization of child poverty refers to the process of getting the problem of child poverty off the residual state's political agenda. Faced with a unanimous 1989 House resolution to take action on child poverty, and with a civil society mobilized around the problem of child poverty, the residual state acted on two fronts. First, the nature of the problem was reframed from a structural to a moral issue, and with this reframing, moral responsibility for its solution was shifted from the state to civil society. Second, the role of the state in rehabilitating the parents of poor children—which essentially referred to promoting their labour force participation—had both moral justification and ideological consistency.

From Entitlement to Charity

Social policy reform and the normalization of child poverty are closely inter-related processes in the transition from the welfare state to the residual state. These processes paved the way in the transition from entitlement to charity as a solution to the problem of child poverty that the Canadian state was committed to by the 1989 House of Commons resolution. How has the residual state faired on this resolution? According to Campaign 2000's report card for 2005,[3] 1.2 million children live in poverty in Canada—compared to 936,000 in 1989. Despite economic growth, the child poverty rate has stuck at around 18 percent since 2000—compared to 12.6 percent in 1989. Thus, while the transition of social policy from entitlement to charity seems to be almost seamless, clearly the state has not met the challenge of the 1989 resolution. How has it faired on the goal of making public welfare more efficient? While this can be assessed from many dimensions, one clear implication of the efficiency promise is to make public welfare more financially efficient.

In this context, the question is whether downloading responsibility for child poverty onto the voluntary sector has resulted in a reduction of federal expenditures on social policy. While the residual state was not fully developed until 2000, Chapter Four used a linear regression model to explore the relationship between federal expenditures on social policy and child poverty in the welfare state, 1971–81, and in the transition to the residual state, 1985–95. The regression revealed that there was a strong negative correlation between state expenditure on social policy and child poverty in the welfare state. In other words, as federal expenditure on social policy increased, child poverty decreased (or vice-versa). In contrast, in the 1985–95 period, there was a moderate positive correlation between federal expenditure on social policy and child poverty. In other words, they tended to increase or decrease in tandem, reflecting that the federal role in social policy had indeed been broken. The fact that child poverty has continued to increase is a reflection on the residual state at both the federal and provincial levels, and a reflection on the residual model of welfare benefits.

1 The Problem of Child Poverty in Canada

1. Susan McClelland, "Child Poverty: We Pledged to Eliminate it. So What Happened?" *MacLean's*, 17 September 2001.
2. The concept of discourse relates to a formal presentation prepared for communicating something through language. Composed of statements of fact, interpretation and judgment, a discourse presents a perspective or point of view that is more or less authoritative, depending on the role, status and power of the communicator. Discourse, in effect, constitutes a tool of ideology.
3. Wanda Wiegers, *The Framing of Poverty as "Child Poverty" and its Implications for Women* (Government of Canada: SW21–94/2002E–IN, June 2002), 6.
4. The major national coalitions include Campaign 2000, www.campaign2000.ca; Canadian Coalition for the Rights of Children, www.rightsofchildren.ca, similar to Campaign 2000 but with an international focus; Campaign Against Child Poverty, www.childpoverty. com; National Children's Alliance, www.nationalchildrensalliance.com; Citizens for Public Justice, www.cpj.ca/action/child_pov.html;. Government of Canada Social Union Initiative, http://socialunion.gc.ca; PovNet, www.povnet.web.net; National Anti-Poverty Organization, www.napo-onap.ca; First Call, www.sunnyhill.bc.ca/first_call; The Progress of Canada's Children, www.ccsd.ca/pcc98/pcc98.htm.
5. Campaign 2000, "Introduction to Campaign 2000," www.campaign2000.ca/about.
6. Campaign 2000, "More than 1.1 million children living in poverty," www.campagin2000. ca/rc/rc02/l.html, (accessed 6 May 2003).
7. See for example Human Resources Development Canada, Applied Research Branch research themes and publications, www.hdrc-drhc.gc.ca/sp-ps/ab-dgra.
8. See for example the publications (especially those related to child poverty and family) of the Canadian Council on Social Development, www.ccsd.ca; The Caledon Institute on Social Policy, www.caledoninst.org; The Vanier Institute of the Family, www.vifamily. ca; The Laidlaw Foundation, www.laidlawfdn.org; Centre for Families, Work and Well-Being, www.worklifecanada.ca; Canadian Centre for Studies of Children at Risk, www-fhs. mcmaster.ca/cscr; Canadian Policy Research Network, www.cprn.org.
9. National Council of Welfare, *Child Poverty Profile 1998* 114 (Summer 2001), Minister of Public Works and Government Services, H68–52/1998E, 1.
10. Leslie Stevenson, *Seven Theories of Human Nature*, 2nd ed. (New York: Oxford University Press, 1987).

11. Also Vic George and Paul Wilding, *Ideology and Social Welfare* (London: Routledge & Kegan Paul, 1985); Angela Djao, *Inequality and Social Policy: The Sociology of Welfare* (Toronto: Wiley, 1983); Robert Mullaly, *Structural Social Work: Ideology, Theory and Practice,* 2nd ed. (Toronto: Oxford University Press, 1997).

12. While different labels were used by the different authors, their categories are congruent.

13. M. Reitsma-Street, R. Carriere, A.Van de Sande, and C. Hein, "Three Perspectives on Child Poverty," *The Social Worker* 61, no. 1 (Spring 1993): 6–12.

14. UNICEF Innocenti Research Center, *Overview,* www.unicef-icdc.org/aboutIRC.

15. See www.unicef-icdc.org/cgi-bin/unicef series for publications information and list.

16. UNICEF Innocenti Research Center, *Children in industrialized countries: Report cards on children in industrialized countries,* www.unicef-icdc.org/research/ESP/CHCl.htm.

17. UNICEF, *A league table of child poverty in rich nations. Innocenti Report Card* No. 1, (June 2000): 3, www.unicef-icdc.org.

18. Ibid.

19. UNICEF Innocenti Research Center, *A league table of child deaths by injury in rich nations. Innocenti Report Card,* No. 2 (February 2001): 14.

20. Ibid., 16–17.

21. OECD web homepage, www.oecd.org/home.

22. The Secretariat, *Beyond 2000: The New Social Policy Agenda, Socio-Economic Change and Social Policy,* OECD/GD(96)170 (Paris: OECD Head of Publications Service, 1996).

23. Jean-Marc Burniaux, Thai-Thanh Dang, Douglas Fore, Michael Forster, Marco Mira d'Ercole and Howard Oxley, *Income Distribution and Poverty in Selected OECD Countries,* Economics Department Working Papers No. 189 (OECD: www.oecd.org/dataoecd/34/37/1864447.pdf).

24. See, for example, Pablo Antolin, Thai-Thanh Dang and Howard Oxley, *Poverty Dynamics in Four OECD Countries,* Economics Department Working Paper No. 212 (OECD: www.oecd.org/dataoecd/57/21/1808105.pdf). A study that includes Canada as one of the four countries.

25. Maryanne Webber, *Measuring Low Income and Poverty in Canada: An Update* (May 1998), Statistics Canada, 98–13, 1–3.

26. Bernard Paquet, *Low Income Cutoffs from 1990 to 1999 and Low Income Measures from 1989 to 1998* (January 2001), Statistics Canada, 75F000MIE–00017, 9–10.

27. For a review of public discourse on the nature and measurement of poverty in the 1960s influencing Statistics Canada's formulation of LICO, see K.M. Lederer, *The Nature of Poverty: An Interpretative Review of Poverty Studies, with Special Reference to Canada,* Human Resources Research Council, 1972, 23–37.

28. Paquet, *Low Income Cutoffs,* 10. This publication provides details on the methods used to calculate low-income cut-offs.

29. Ibid., 17. The after-tax LICOs were derived independently and calculated separately from pre-tax LICOs and had "no simple relationship...that distinguishes the two levels."

30. Cathy Cotton, *Should the Low Income Cutoffs be Updated? A Discussion Paper* (December 1999), Statistics Canada, 75F002MIE–99009, 24–25.

31. Webber, *Measuring Low Income,* 7.

32. Ibid.

33. Canadian Council on Social Development, *The Canadian Fact Book on Poverty 2000,* 35–37; Cathy Cotton, Maryanne Webber, and Y. Saint-Pierre, *Should the Low Income Cut-offs be Updated? A Discussion Paper* (Ottawa: Statistics Canada, 1999).

34. Paquet, *Low Income Cutoffs,* 17.

35. Webber, *Measuring Low Income,* 7.

36. Christopher Sarlo, *Poverty in Canada* (Vancouver: The Fraser Institute, 1992).

37. HDRC, "The Market Basket Measure Constructing a New Measure of Poverty," *Applied Research Bulletin* 4, no. 2 (Summer/Fall 1998), www.hdrc.ca.

38. Ibid.

39. Cotton, *Should the Low Income Cut-offs be Updated?,* 25.

40. Standing Senate Committee on Social Affairs, Science and Technology, *Children in Poverty: Toward a Better Future.* A report presented at the 34th Parliament, 2nd Session, 1.

41. Ibid., 3.

42. *Developments* 1, no. 1 (April 1995), the inaugural edition of the NLSCY newsletter, www. hrdc-drhc.gc.ca/sp-ps/arb-dgra/nlscy-elnej/news-nouvelles.

43. *Developments* 2, no. 2 (October 1996), www.hrdc-drhc.gc.ca/sp-ps/arb-dgra/nlscy-elnej/ news-nouvelles.

44. *Developments* 3, no. 1 (March 1998), www.hrdc-drhc.gc.ca/sp-ps/arb-dgra/nlscy-elnej/ news-nouvelles.

45. National Children's Agenda, "Background Information on Centres of Excellence for Children's Well-being," www.socialunion.gc.ca/nca/nca3_e (accessed 16 February 2004).

46. Health Canada, "Government of Canada Announces Five Centres of Excellence for Children's Well-Being," News Releases 5 October 2000 (2000–97), www.hc-sc.gc.ca/ english/media/releases/2000.

47. J. Douglas Willms, ed., *Vulnerable Children: Findings from Canada's National Longitudinal Survey of Children and Youth* (Edmonton: University of Alberta Press, 2002), xii.

48. Ibid.

49. Ibid., 8.

50. Gary Teeple, *Globalization and the Decline of Social Reform* (Aurora: Garamon Books, 2000)

51. Dennis Guest, *The Emergence of Social Security in Canada,* 2nd ed. (Vancouver: University of British Columbia Press, 1985), 5–8.

2 *The Canadian Welfare State and the Growth of Entitlement*

1. P. Springborg, *The Problem of Human Needs and the Critique of Civilization* (London: Allen & Unwin, 1981).

2. Richard Titmus, *Commitment to Welfare* (London: Allen & Unwin, 1976), 188.

3. C.B. Macpherson, "Needs and Wants: An ontological or historical problem?" in *Human Needs and Politics,* ed. Ross Fitzgerald (New York: Pergamon Press, 1977), 26–35.

4. Ibid., 28.

5. Ibid., 31.

6. Ibid., 32.

7. Ibid.

8. See, for example, Kai Nielsen, "True Needs, Rationality and Emancipation," in *Human Needs and Politics,* ed. Ross Fitzgerarld, 142–56; and Agnes Heller, *The Theory of Need in Marx* (London: Allison & Busby, 1974).

9. P. Springborg, *The Problem of Human Needs and the Critique of Civilization* (London: Allen & Unwin, 1981), 162–63.

10. Ross Fitzgerald, "Abraham Maslow's Hierarchy of Needs—An Exposition and Evaluation" in *Human Needs and Politics* ed. Ross Fitzgerald.

11. Ibid., 37–46.

12. Vic George and Paul Wilding, *Ideology and Social Welfare* (London: Routledge & Kegan Paul, 1985).

13. Ibid., 123.

14. Ibid., 123–24.

15. Richard Simeon, *In Search of a Social Contract: Can We Make Hard Decisions as if Democracy Matters?* (C.D. Howe Institute, Benefactors Lecture, 1994), 15–19.

16. Ibid.

17. Ibid., 17.

18. Ibid., 18.

19. Shankar Yelaja, "Canadian Social Policy: Perspectives," in *Canadian Social Policy,* ed. Shankar Yelaja (Waterloo: Wilfrid Laurier University Press, 1978), 1–26.

20. Gregg M. Olsen, "Locating the Canadian Welfare State: Family Policy and Health Care in Canada, Sweden and the United States," in *Power Resources Theory and the Welfare State,* eds. Julia S. O'Connor and Gregg M. Olsen (Toronto: University of Toronto Press, 1998), 6.

21. Leonard Marsh, *Report on Social Security for Canada* (Toronto: University of Toronto Press, 1975), 21–22.

22. Ibid., 4.

23. Michael Bliss, "Preface," in *Report on Social Security for Canada,* Leonard Marsh.

24. Dennis Guest, *The Emergence of Social Security in Canada,* 2nd ed. (Vancouver: University of British Columbia Press, 1985), 107.

25. Leslie A. Pal, "Revision and Retreat: Canadian Unemployment Insurance, 1971–1981," in *Canadian Social Welfare Policy: Federal and Provincial Dimensions,* ed. Jacqueline S. Ismael (Kingston: McGill-Queen's University Press, 1985), 77.

26. Guest, *The Emergence of Social Security,* 108.

27. "The federal government passed legislation in 1944 to introduce family allowances, for each child up to 16 years of age, funded from general revenue and in 1948, it introduced several federal grants under orders-in-council to support the development of provincial health services." R. Robinson, Health and Welfare Canada, 11–516–XIE *Historical Statistics of Canada,* www.statcan.ca/english/freepub/11–516–XIE/sectionc/sectionc.htm.

28. Guest, *The Emergence of Social Security,* 128–33.

29. John C. Bacher, *Keeping to the Marketplace: The Evolution of Canadian Housing Policy* (Montreal: McGill-Queen's University Press, 1993), 3.

30. W. Edward Mann, *Poverty and social policy in Canada.* (Vancouver: The Copp Clark Publishing Co., 1970), vii.

31. Guest, *The Emergence of Social Security,* 155.

32. Derek J. Hum, *Federalism and the Poor: A Review of the Canada Assistance Plan* (Toronto: Ontario Economic Council, 1983), 32.

33. R. S. Haddow, *Poverty Reform in Canada, 1958–1978* (Montreal: McGill-Queen's University Press, 1993), 59.

34. As quoted in Guest, *The Emergence of Social Security,* 151.

35. Ibid., 154.

36. Economic Council of Canada, "The Challenge of Growth and Change," in chap. 6 of *Fifth Annual Review* (Ottawa: Queen's Printer, 1968).

37. Special Senate Committee on Poverty, *Poverty in Canada* (Ottawa: Supply and Services Canada, 1973), vi.

38. J. C. Bacher, *Keeping to the Marketplace: The Evolution of Canadian Housing Policy* (Montreal: McGill-Queen's University Press, 1993), 245.

39. Special Senate Committee on Poverty, *Poverty in Canada* (Ottawa: Supply and Services Canada, 1976), 18–20.

40. Ibid., 23.

41. Ibid., xxi–xxiii.

42. Adams, Ian, William Cameron, Brian Hill and Peter Penz, *The Real Poverty Report* (Edmonton: Hurtig, 1971).

43. Ibid., vi.

44. Ibid.

45. Haddow, *Poverty Reform in Canada,* 89.

46. Lalonde, M. *Working paper on social security in Canada,* 2nd ed. (Ottawa: Government of Canada, 1973), 4.

47. J. Muszynski, "Social Policy and Canadian Federalism: What are the Pressures for Change?" in *New Trends in Canadian Federalism,* eds. F. Rocher and M. Smith (Petersborough: Broadview Press), 295.

48. Haddow, *Poverty Reform in Canada,* 20–163.

49. Ibid., 163

50. Discussed earlier in the chapter.

51. R. Mishra, *The Welfare State in Crisis* (New York: Harvester Wheatsheaf, 1994), 42.

52. Linda McQuaig, *Shooting the Hippo: Death by Deficit and Other Canadian Myths* (Toronto: Viking, 1995), 5.

53. Daniel Cohn, "The Canada Health and Social Transfer: Transferring Resources or Moral Authority Between Levels of Government?" in *Canada the State of the Federation: 1996.* eds. Patrick Fafard and Douglas Brown (Kingston, Canada: Queen's University Institute of Intergovernmental Relations, 1996), 172.

54. Amendments to Canada Pension Plan, 1965 to 1987.
    Between 1965 through to 1986
    • introduction of full annual cost-of-living indexation;
    • introduction of the same benefits to male and female contributors as well as their surviving spouses and dependent children;
    • removal of the retirement and employment earnings test for retirement pensions at 65 years of age;
    • elimination of periods of zero or low earnings while caring for a child under the age of seven; and
    • splitting of pension credits between spouses if there is a divorce or separation.
    1987
    • flexible retirement benefits payable at 60 years of age;
    • greater disability pension;
    • extension of survivor's benefits if spouse remarries;
    • sharing retirement pensions between spouses;
    • growth of credit splitting to cover the separation of married or common-law spouses.

55. R. Simeon and I. Robinson, *State, Society, and the Development of Canadian Federalism* (Toronto: University of Toronto Press, 1990).

56. Ibid., 24.

57. Ibid., 59.

58. P. Barker, "Disentangling the Federation: Social Policy and Fiscal Federalism," in *Challenges to Canadian Federalism,* eds. M. Westmacott and H. Mellon (Scarborough: Prentice Hall Canada), 144.

95

59. Keith Banting, *The Welfare State and Canadian Federalism*, 2nd ed. (Kingston: McGill-Queen's University Press), 174.

60. Ibid.,176.

61. Ibid., 177.

62. G. Stevenson, "The Origins of Co-operative Federalism," in *Federalism and Political Community: Essays in Honour of Donald Smiley,* eds. D. Shugarman and R. Whitaker (Peterborough: Broadview Press, 1989), 7.

63. As quoted in Richard Simeon, *In Search of a Social Contract: Can We Make Hard Decisions as if Democracy Matters?* (C.D. Howe Institute, Benefactors Lecture, 1994), 157.

64. D. Smiley, *Canada in Question: Federalism in the Eighties,* 3rd ed. (Toronto: McGraw-Hill Ryerson, 1980), 91.

65. As quoted in R. Watts, "Executive federalism: The comparative perspective," in *Federalism and Political Community,* eds. D. Shugarman, and R. Whitaker (Peterborough, ON: Broadview Press Ltd., 1989), 440.

66. Ibid.

67. See Appendix Table D.

68. W. Wiegers, "The Framing of Poverty as 'Child Poverty' and its Implications for Women" (Government of Canada: Cat. No. SW21–94–2002E-IN), 18–20.

3 *The Residual State and the Mobilization of Charity*

1. The policy accommodation and accommodation of values that buttressed the welfare state were based on Keynesian demand-side economics and had already been eroded by the onset of stagflation (as discussed in Chapter Two).

2. See Bruce Headey, ed., *Real World of Welfare Capitalism* (Cambridge University Press, 1999); Bernhard Ebbinghaus, ed., *Comparing Welfare Capitalism: Social Policy & Political Economy in Europe, Japan, & the USA* (London: Routledge & Kegan Paul, 2001); and Keith Banting, "Social Policy Challenges in a Global Society," in *Social Policy in a Global Society* (Ottawa: IDRC, 1996); Gary Teeple, *Globalization and the Decline of Social Reform* (Aurora: Garamond Press, 2000).

3. 1992 Charlottetown Accord, www.ola.bc.ca/online/cf/documents/ 1992CHARLOTTETOWN.html.

4. Human Resources Development Canada, *Improving Social Security in Canada: A Discussion Paper,* cat. no. SC–035–09–94F.

5. Daniel Cohn, "The Canada health and social transfer: Transferring resources or moral authority between levels of government?" in *Canada the State of the Federation: 1996,* eds. Patrick Fafard and Douglas Brown (Kingston, Canada: Queen's University Institute of Intergovernmental Relations, 1996), 172.

6. Department of Human Resources Development Act (1996, c. 11).

7. News Release, "First Meeting of Federal-Provincial-Territorial Council on Social Policy Renewal," November 27, 1996, www.socialunion.gc.ca/news/96nov27c.html, (accessed 14 February 2004).

8. News Release, "Federal/Provincial/Territorial Ministers Responsible for Social Services get to work on National Child Benefit," 19 February 1997, www.nationalchildbenefit.ca/ ncb/news/, (accessed 14 February 2004).

9. Benefits and Services for Persons with Disabilities, "Employability Assistance for People with Disabilities," http://socialunion.gc.pwd (accessed April 2004).

10. Ministers Responsible for Social Services, *Employability Assistance for People with Disabilities, May 2002* (Ottawa: Human Resources Development Canada, SDDP–030–05–02E, 2002), 3.

11. National Childcare Benefit Website, "A unique partnership of the Government of Canada, Provinces and Territories and First Nations," www.nationalchildbenefit.ca/ncb, (accessed 16 February 2004).

12. News Release, "Federal-Provincial-Territorial Meeting of Ministers Responsible for Social Services," 12 March 1998, www.socialunion.gc.ca/news/98march12e.html, (accessed 17 February 2004).

13. National Council of Welfare, *Fact Sheet: Welfare Recipients,* www.newcnbes.net/htmdocument/principales/numberwelfare (accessed 16 February 2004).

14. See Chapter One.

15. Speech from the Throne, 23 September 1997, www.socialunion.gc.ca/nca.

16. Federal-Provincial-Territorial Council of Ministers on Social Policy Renewal, *Public Report: Public Dialogue on the National Children's Agenda—Developing a Shared Vision,* June 2000, http://socialunion.gc.ca/nca/June21-2000 (accessed 17 February 2004).

17. News Release, "Council on Social Policy Renewal Launches Work on Framework Agreement for Canada's Social Union," 13 March 1998, http://socialunion.gc.ca/news/98mar13c.html.

18. Harvey Lazar, "The Social Union Framework Agreement: Lost Opportunity or New Beginning?" School of Policy Studies, *Working Paper 3* (August 2000), 1.

19. "A Framework to Improve the Social Union for Canadians: An Agreement between the Government of Canada and the Governments of the Provinces and Territories," 4 February 1999, Article 5, http://socialunion.gc.ca (accessed 1 April 2004).

20. Ibid.

21. Government of Canada, *Early Childhood Development Activities and Expenditures, 2002–2003* (Ottawa: Human Resources Development Canada, 2003), 1. The provinces and territories were responsible for providing services to children under six and their families under their jurisdiction, First Nation and Inuit children and their families fell under federal jurisdiction; also children under six and their families on Canadian military bases.

22. See Chapter One.

23. For a list of provincial services available by province see www1.servicecanada.gc.ca/en/gateways/where_you_live/menu.shtml.

24. Government of Canada, *Early Childhood Development Activities and Expenditures, 2000–2001* (cat. no. H21-183-2002), http://socialunion.gc.ca/ecd/toc_e.html.

25. Ibid., 67. The provinces and territories were responsible for providing services to children under six and their families under their jurisdiction; First Nation and Inuit children and their families fell under federal jurisdiction; also children under six and their families on Canadian military bases.

26. Government of Canada, "Baseline Report on Early Learning and Child Care," chap. 8 in *Early Childhood Development Activities and Expenditures, 2002-2003,* (http://socialunion.gc.ca/ccd/2003/report1_e/chapter08_e,htm (accessed March 2004).

27. Voluntary Sector Initiate (VSI) website, "About the VSI" www.vsi-isbc.ca/eng/about, (accessed April 2004).

28. Jacqueline S. Ismael, "Privatization of Social Services: A Heuristic Approach," in *Privatization and Provincial Social Services in Canada,* eds. Jacqueline S. Ismael and Yves Vaillancourt (Edmonton: University of Alberta Press, 1988), 5.

29. Voluntary Sector Initiative www.vsi-isbc.ca/eng/index.cfm.

30. The federal government also funds a number of social programs directly through community providers. In the area of health monitoring, promotion and education, for example, in 2001–2002, federal funding in this area for children under six was $183.4 million for 31 health related programs. For program details, see Government of Canada, *Early Childhood Development Activities and Expenditures, 2001–2002* (Cat. No: H21–183/2002).

31. Total income data from: 1951 to 1967, from the Special Senate Committee on Poverty (1971); *Poverty in Canada* (Ottawa: Alger Press Limited, 15); 1978 and 1979 from Statistics Canada, *Income Distributions by Size in Canada, 1997,* cat. no. 13–207–XPB; 1980–1996 from Statistics Canada, Income Distributions by Size in Canada, 1997, cat. no. 13–206 Annual; After-tax Quintile data from Statistics Canada, *Income in Canada, 2002,* cat. no. 75–202–XlE.

32. CANSIM Label D44480.

33. Gillespie, W.I. *In search of Robin Hood: The effect of federal budgetary policies during the 1970s on the distribution of income in Canada.* (Toronto: C.D. Howe Institute, 1978).

34. D. Adamchak, "Emerging trends in the relationship between infant mortality and socioeconomic status," *Social Biology* 26, no.1 (Spring 1979): 16–29; T. LaVeist, "Simulating the effects of poverty on the race disparity in postneonatal mortality," *Journal of Public Health Policy* 11, no. 4 (Winter 1990): 463–73; T. LaVeist, "Segregation, poverty, and empowerment: Health consequences for African Americans," *The Milbank Quarterly* 71, no. 1 (1993): 41–64; K. Newland, K. *Worldwatch Paper 47:* Infant mortality and the health of societies (Washington: Worldwatch Institute, 1980); A. Creighton-Zollar, "Infant mortality by socioeconomic status and race in Richmond, Virginia 1979–1981: A research note," *Sociological Spectrum* 10, no. 1, 1990, 133–42; S. Gortmaker, "Poverty and infant mortality in the United States," *American Sociological Review* 44, no. 2 (April 1979): 280–97; J. Hedderson, and H. Daudistel, "Infant mortality of the Spanish surname population," *The Social Science Journal* 19, no. 4 (October 1982): 67–78; S. Bird, "Separate black and white infant mortality models: Differences in the importance of structural variables," *Social Science and Medicine* 41, no. 11 (December 1995), 1507–12.

35. Standing Senate Committee on Social Affairs, Science and Technology, *Children in poverty: Toward a better future.* A report presented at the 34th Parliament, 2nd session, January 1991, 34.

36. Ibid.

37. D. Malikin, "Research and Rumination," in *Social Disability: Alcoholism, Drug Addiction, Crime and Social Disadvantage,* ed. D. Malikin (New York: New York University Press, 1973), 235.

38. Anon., Canadian children in the 1990s: Selected findings of the national longitudinal survey of children and youth. *Canadian Social Trends* (Spring 1997). (Statistics Canada—Catalogue 11–008–XPE),

39. Kitchen, B., A. Mitchell, P. Clutterbuck, & M. Novick,. *Unequal futures: The legacies of child poverty in Canada.* Toronto: (The Social Planning Council of Metropolitan Toronto, 1991), 7.

40. Standing Committee on Social Affairs, 1991, 36.

41. J. Oderkirk, Food banks. *Canadian social trends* (Spring 1992), 6–7.

42. Ibid., 1992, 7–8.

43. Canadian Association of Food Banks, *Hunger Count 98,* www.icomm.ca/cafb.

44. Ibid.

45. L. McIntyre, S. Connor, and J. Warren, *A Glimpse of Child Hunger in Canada,* (Ottawa: Human Resources Development Canada, 1998), www.hrdc-drhc.gc.ca/arb.

46. Canada, Bureau of Nutritional Sciences, *Nutrition: A National Priority* (Ottawa: Government of Canada, 1975).

47. Anon., Canadian children in the 1990s: Selected findings of the national longitudinal survey of children and youth. *Canadian Social Trends* (Spring 1997). (Statistics Canada—Catalogue 11–008–XPE),1997, 8.

48. J. Oderkirk, Disabilities among children. *Canadian social trend,* Spring 1993, 23.

49. Ibid., 23.

50. Ibid., 25.

51. Ibid.

52. Canadian Teachers' Federation. *Children, schools and poverty.* (Ottawa: Canadian Teachers' Federation, 1990).

4 *Child Poverty and Changing Federal Policy*

1. M. Drolet, "To What Extent are Canadians Exposed to Low Income?" Income Research Paper Series, Statistics Canada, 75F00MIE99001, 1999; Ross Finnie, "An Econometric Analysis of Poverty Dynamics in Canada," Working Paper 9, School of Policy Studies, October 2000; Mireille Laroche, "The Persistence of Low Income Spells in Canada, 1982–1993," Economic Studies and Policy Analysis Division, Department of Finance, September 1997; Howard Oxley, Thai Thanh Dang and Pablo Antolin, "Poverty Dynamics in Six OECD Countries," OECD Economic Studies No. 30, 2000/1 (2000); G. Picot and J. Myles, "Children in Low Income Families," *Canadian Social Trends* (Autumn 1996), Statistics Canada Catalogue 11–008–XPE; G. Picot, M. Zyblock and W. Pyper, "Why Do Children Move into and Out of Low Income: Changing Labour Market Conditions on Marriage and Divorce?" Research Paper Series No. 132; Statistics Canada, 11F0019MPE No. 132, April 1999; D. Ross, R. Shillington and C. Lockhead, *The Canadian Fact Book on Poverty, 1994* (Ottawa: Canadian Council on Social Development, 1996).

2. BC Ministry of Human Recourses, *Your Guide to Employment and Assistance,* www.mhr. gov.bc.ca/publicat/bcea (accessed 17 August 2004).

3. Ibid. (accessed 24 June 2005).

4. BC Ministry of Human Resources, *Time Limits Update,* www.mhr.gov.bc.ca/factsheets/2004 (accessed 17 August 2004).

5. B.C. Ministry of Human Resources, *Update to the Dental Program* www.mhr.bc.ca/factsheets/2004 (accessed 17 August 2004).

6. Ibid. (accessed 24 June 2005).

7. Government of Alberta, Human Resources and Employment, *Income Security* www3.gov. ab.ca/hre/isp (accessed 17 August 2004).

8. Ibid. (accessed 24 June 2005).

9. Ibid.

10. Saskatchewan, *Saskatchewan Assistance Plan,* www.dcre.gov.sk.ca/financial/SAP (accessed 27 August 2004).

11. Ibid. (accessed 24 June 2005).

12. Ibid.

13. National Council of Welfare, *Welfare Incomes,* 2003, 82–83.

14. Manitoba Family Services and housing, *Employment and Income Assistance Program,* www.gov.mb.ca/fs/assistance (accessed 18 August 2004).

15. Ibid. (accessed 24 June 2005).

16. Manitoba Family Services and Housing, *Housing Channel,* www.gov.mb.ca/fs/housing (accessed 18 August 2004).

17. Ontario Ministry of Community and Social Services, *Ontario Works,* www.cvcs.gov.on.ca/CFCS/en/programs (accessed 24 August 2004).

18. Ontario Ministry of Municipal Affairs and Housing, *Social Housing Reform Legislation,* www.mah.gov.on.ca/scripts (accessed 24 August 2004).

19. Ontario Housing Corporation, *Assessment of Capital Funding Models Within the Context of Social Housing Devolution,* October 2000, www.mah.gov.on.ca/userfiles/HTML (accessed 24 August 2004).

20. Government of Quebec, *Employment Assistance,* www.mess.gouv.qc.ca/anglais/sr/assistance (accessed 26 August 2004).

21. Ibid. (accessed 24 June 2005).

22. Government of New Brunswick, *Family Income Security Act,* www.gnb.ca/0017/Policy%20Manual (accessed 19 August 2004).

23. New Brunswick Regulation 95–61, www.gnb.ca/0017/Policy%20Manual/POL-E/menu16.htm (accessed 19 August 2004).

24. Ibid. (accessed 24 June 2005).

25. New Brunswick Department of Family and Community Services, *Housing Programs,* www.gnb.ca/0017/Housing (accessed 19 August 2004).

26. New Brunswick Department of Family and Community Services, 2002–2003 Annual Report, www.gnb.ca/0017/publications, (accessed 19 August 2004).

27. Newfoundland and Labrador Human Resources, Labour and Employment, *Income Support—Frequently Asked Questions,* www.gov.nf.ca/hre/incsppt (accessed 22 August 2004).

28. Newfoundland and Labrador Housing Corporation, Housing Programs, www.nlhc.nf.ca/programs (accessed 22 August 2004).

39. Nova Scotia Department of Community Services, *Employment Support and Community Assistance,* www.gov.ns.ca/coms, (accessed 23 August 2004).

30. Nova Scotia Department of Community Services, *Nova Scotia Employment Support and Income Assistance Manual,* www.gov.ns.ca/coms (accessed 23 August 2004).

31. Government of Prince Edward Island, PEI Social Assistance Policy Manual, www.gov.pe.ca/infopei (accessed 25 August 2004).

5   *Social Policy Reform and the Normalization of Child Poverty*

1. See Table 1–1: Ideological Perspectives, in Chapter One.

2. See www.brainydictionary.com/words.

3. Campaign 2000, *2005 Report Card on Child Poverty in Canada,* www.campaign2000.ca.

Bibliography

Adamchak, D. (1979, Spring). Emerging trends in the relationship between infant mortality and socioeconomic status. *Social Biology, 26* (1), 16–29.

Adams, I., Cameron, W., Hill, B. & Penz, P. (1971). *The real poverty report.* Edmonton: Hurtig.

Anon, Canadian children in the 1990s: Selected findings of the national longitudinal survey of children and youth. *Canadian Social Trends* (Spring 1997). Statistics Canada — Catalogue 11–008–XPE.

Antolin, P., Thai-Thanh Dang & Oxley, H. (1999). *Poverty dynamics in four OECD countries,* Economics Department Working Paper No. 212 (OECD: ECO/WKP(99)).

Bacher, J.C. (1993). *Keeping to the marketplace: The evolution of Canadian housing policy.* Montreal: McGill-Queen's University Press.

Banting, K. (1987). The welfare state and Canadian Federalism (2nd. ed.). Kingston: McGill-Queen's University Press.

———. (1996). Social policy challenges in a global society. In D. Morales-Gómez and Mario Torres A. *Social Policy in a Global Society.* Ottawa: IDRC.

Barker, P. (1998). Disentangling the federation: Social policy and fiscal federalism. In M. *Westmacott & H. Mellon (Eds.), Challenges to Canadian Federalism,* (144–156). Scarborough: Prentice Hall Canada.

Battle, K. (1998, December). Transformation: Canadian social policy since 1985. *Social Policy & Administration,* 32(4), 321–340.

Bird, S. (1995, December). Separate black and white infant mortality models: Differences in the importance of structural variables. *Social Science and Medicine, 41* (11), 1507–1512.

Bliss, M. (1975). Preface. In Marsh, L. (Ed.), *Report on social security for Canada.* Toronto: University of Toronto Press.

Boychuk, G. W. (2004, Winter). Asymmetry and Paradox: Social Policy and the U.S-Canada Bilateral Relationship. *American Review of Canadian Studies,* 34(4), 689–701.

Burniaux, J.-M., Thai-Thanh Dang, Fore, D., Forster, M., Mira d'Ercole , M., & Oxley, H. (1998). *Income distribution and poverty in selected OECD countries.* Economics Department Working Papers No. 189 (OECD: ECO/WKP(2)). Canada (1975).

Bureau of Nutritional Sciences (1973). *Nutrition: A National Priority.* Ottawa: Government of Canada.

Cohn, D. (1996). The Canada health and social transfer: Transferring resources or moral authority between levels of government? In P. Fafard & D. Brown (Eds.), *Canada the State of the Federation: 1996* (172). Kingston, Canada: Queen's University Institute of Intergovernmental Relations.

Cotton, C. *Should the low income cutoffs be updated? A discussion paper.* Statistics Canada: 75F0002MIE–99009.

Cotton, C., Webber, M. & Saint-Pierre, Y. (1999). *Should the low income cut-offs be updated? A discussion paper.* Ottawa: Statistics Canada.

Creighton-Zollar, A. (1990). Infant mortality by socioeconomic status and race in Richmond, Virginia 1979–1981: A research note. *Sociological Spectrum, 10* (1), 133–142.

Djao, A. (1983). *Inequality and social policy: The sociology of welfare.* Toronto: Wiley.

Drolet, M. (1999). To What Extent are Canadians Exposed to Low Income? Income Research Paper Series. Statistics Canada. (cat. 75F00MIE99001).

Ebbinghaus, B. (Ed.). (2001). *Comparing welfare capitalism: Social policy & political economy in Europe, Japan, & the USA.* New York: Routledge.

Economic Council of Canada. (1968). The challenge of growth and change. In *Fifth Annual Review* (Chapter 6). Ottawa: Queen's Printer.

Finnie, R. (2000, October). An econometric analysis of poverty dynamics in Canada. School of Policy Studies, Working Paper 9.

Fitzgerald, R. (1977). Abraham Maslow's hierarchy of needs—An exposition and evaluation. In R. Fitzgerald (Ed.), *Human needs and politics.* New York: Pergamon Press.

George, V., & Wilding, P. (1985). *Ideology and social welfare.* London: Routledge & Kegan Paul.

Gillespie, W.I. (1978). *In search of Robin Hood: The effect of federal budgetary policies during the 1970s on the distribution of income in Canada.* Toronto: C.D. Howe Institute.

Gortmaker, S. (1979, April). Poverty and infant mortality in the United States. *American Sociological Review, 44* (2), 280–297.

Government of Canada. (2003). *Early childhood development activities and expenditures, 2002–2003.* Ottawa: Human Resources Development Canada.

Government of Canada. (2002). *Early childhood development activities and expenditures, 2001–2002.* (cat. no: H21–183/2002).

Graham, J., Swift, K. & Delaney, R. (2003). *Canadian social policy: An introduction* (2nd ed.). Toronto: Prentice Hall.

Guest, D. (1985). *The emergence of social security in Canada* (2nd ed.). Vancouver: University of British Columbia.

Haddow, R. S. (1993). *Poverty reform in Canada, 1958–1978.* Montreal: McGill-Queen's University Press.

Headey, B. (Ed.). (1999). *Real world of welfare capitalism.* New York: Cambridge University Press.

Hedderson, J., & Daudistel, H. (1982, October). Infant mortality of the Spanish surname population. *The Social Science Journal, 19* (4), 67–78.

Heller, A. (1976) *The theory of need in Marx.* London: Allison & Busby.

Heinonen, T., MacKay, I., Metteri, A., & Pajula, M.-L. (2001). Social work and health restructuring in Canada and Finland. *Social Work in Health Care, 34*(1/2), 71–87.

Hum, D. J. (1983). *Federalism and the poor: A review of the Canada Assistance Plan.* Toronto: Ontario Economic Council.

Human Resources Development Canada. (2002). *Improving social security in Canada: A discussion paper.* (cat. no. SC–035–09–94F).

Ismael, J. S. (1988). Privatization of social services: A heuristic approach. In J. S. Ismael & Y. Vaillancourt (Eds.), *Privatization and provincial social services in Canada.* Edmonton: University of Alberta Press.

———— (Ed.). (1988) *Canadian welfare state: Evolution and transition*. Edmonton: The University of Alberta Press.

Kitchen, B., Mitchell, A., Clutterbuck, P., & Novick, M. (1991). *Unequal futures: The legacies of child poverty in Canada*. Toronto: The Social Planning Council of Metropolitan Toronto.

Lalonde, M. (1973). Working paper on social security in Canada (2nd ed.). Ottawa: Government of Canada.

Laroche, M. (1997, September). *The persistence of low income spells in Canada, 1982–1993*. Economic Studies and Policy Analysis Division, Department of Finance.

LaVeist, T. (1990, Winter). Simulating the effects of poverty on the race disparity in postneonatal mortality. *Journal of Public Health Policy, 11* (4), 463–473.

————. (1993). Segregation, poverty, and empowerment: health consequences for African Americans. *The Milbank Quarterly, 71* (1), 41–64.

Lazar, H. (2000, August). The social union framework agreement: Lost opportunity or new beginning?, *School of Policy Studies, Working Paper 3*.

Lederer, K. M. (1972). *The nature of poverty: An interpretative review of poverty studies, with special reference to Canada*. Human Resources Research Council.

Little, M. (2001). A Litmus test for democracy: The impact of Ontario welfare changes on single mothers. *Studies in Political Economy*, (66), 9–36.

MacDonald, M. (1998, December). The impact of a restructured Canadian welfare state on Atlantic Canada. *Social Policy & Administration, 32* (4), 389–400.

Macpherson, C.B. (1977). Needs and wants: An ontological or historical problem? In R. Fitzgerald (Ed.), *Human needs and politics* (26–35). New York: Pergamon Press.

Malikin, D. (1973). Research and rumination. In D. Malikin (Ed.), *Social disability: alcoholism, drug addiction, crime and social disadvantage*. New York: New York University Press.

Mann, W. E. (Ed.). (1970). *Poverty and social policy in Canada*. Vancouver: Copp Clark Publishing.

Marsh, L. (1975). *Report on social security for Canada*. Toronto: University of Toronto Press.

McClelland, S. (2001, September 17). Child poverty: We pledged to eliminate it. So what happened?, *MacLean's*.

McIntyre, L., Connor, S., & Warren, J. (1998). *A glimpse of child hunger in Canada*. Ottawa: Human Resources Development Canada. www.hrdc-drhc.gc.ca/arb

McQuaig, L. (1995). *Shooting the hippo: Death by deficit and other Canadian myths*. Toronto: Viking.

Ministers Responsible for Social Services. (2002, May). *Employability assistance for people with disabilities*. SDDP–030–05–02E. Ottawa: Human Resources Development Canada.

Mishra, R. (1984). *The welfare state in crisis*. New York: Harvester Wheatsheaf.

————. (1987). Public policy and social welfare: The ideology and practice of restraint in Ontario. In J. S. Ismael (Ed.), *The Canadian welfare state: Evolution and transition*. Edmonton: University of Alberta Press.

Mullaly, R. (1997). *Structural social work: Ideology, theory and practice* (2nd ed.). Toronto: Oxford University Press.

Muszynski, J. (1995). Social policy and Canadian federalism: What are the pressures for change? In F. Rocher & M. Smith (Eds.), *New trends in Canadian federalism*. (288–318). Petersborough: Broadview Press.

National Council of Welfare. (2001, Summer). *Child Poverty Profile 1998* (Vol. 114). Minister of Public Works and Government Services. (cat. no. H68–52/1998E).

Nielsen, Kai. (1977). True needs, rationality and emancipation. In R. Fitzgerarld (Ed.), *Human Needs and* Politics (142–156). New York: Pergamon Press.

Newland, K. (1981). *Worldwatch Paper 47: Infant mortality and the health of societies.* Washington: Worldwatch Institute.

Oderkirk, J. (1992) Food banks. *Canadian social trends* (Spring),

Oderkirk, J. (1993). Disabilities among children. *Canadian social trends.* (Winter).

Olsen, G.M. (1998). Locating the Canadian welfare state: Family policy and health care in Canada, Sweden and the United States. In J. S. O'Connor & G. M. Olsen (Eds.), *Power resources theory and the welfare state.* Toronto: University of Toronto Press.

Oxley, H., Thai Thanh Dang & Antolin, P. (2000). Poverty dynamics in six OECD Countries. OECD Economic Studies No. 30, 2000/1.

Pal, L.A. (1985). "Revision and retreat: Canadian Unemployment Insurance, 1971–1981." In J. S. Ismael (Ed.), *Canadian social welfare policy: Federal and provincial dimensions.* Kingston: McGill-Queen's University Press.

Paquet, B. (2001, January). *Low income cutoffs from 1990 to 1999 and low income measures from 1989 to 1998.* Statistics Canada. (75F000MIE-00017).

Picot, G. & Myles, J. (1996, Autumn). "Children in low income families." *Canadian Social Trends*, Statistics Canada (Catalogue 11-008-XPE).

Picot, G., Zyblock, M., &. Pyper, W. (1999, April). "Why do children move into and out of low income: Changing labour market conditions or marriage and divorce?" Statistics Canada Research Paper Series No. 132; (11F0019MPE No. 132).

Prince, M. J. (1998). "Holes in the safety net, leaks in the roof: Changes in Canadian welfare policy and their implications for social housing programs." *Housing Policy Debate 9 (4), 825–848.*

Reitsma-Street, M., Carriere, R., Van de Sande, A., & Hein, C. (1993, Spring). *Three perspectives on child poverty. The Social Worker,* 61(1).

Rice, J.R., & Prince, M. J. (1999). *Changing politics of Canadian social policy.* Toronto: University of Toronto Press.

Ross, D., Shillington, R., & Lockhead, C. (1996). *The Canadian fact book on poverty, 1994.* Ottawa: Canadian Council on Social Development.

Ross, D.P., Scott, K.J. & Smith, P.J. (2000). *The Canadian fact book on poverty 2000.* Ottawa: Canadian Council on Social Development.

Sarlo, C. (1992). *Poverty in Canada.* Vancouver: The Fraser Institute.

Simeon, R. (1994). *In Search of a Social Contract: Can We Make Hard Decisions as if Democracy Matters?* C.D. Howe Institute, Benefactors Lecture.

Simeon, R., & Robinson, I. (1990). *State, society, and the development of Canadian federalism.* Toronto: University of Toronto Press.

Smiley, D. (1980). *Canada in question: Federalism in the eighties* (3rd ed.). Toronto: McGraw-Hill Ryerson.

Special Senate Committee on Poverty. (1971). *Poverty in Canada.* Ottawa: Alger Press Limited.

———. (1973). *Poverty in Canada* (vi). Ottawa: Supply and Services Canada.

Springborg, P. (1981). *The problem of human needs and the critique of civilization.* London: Allen & Unwin.

Standing Senate Committee on Social Affairs, Science and Technology. (1991, January). *Children in poverty: Toward a better future.* A report presented at the 34th Parliament, 2nd Session.

Stevenson, G. (1989). The origins of co-operative federalism. In D. Shugarman & R. Whitaker (Eds.), *Federalism and political community: Essays in honour of Donald Smiley* (7–32). Peterborough: Broadview Press.

Stevenson, L. (1987). *Seven theories of human nature* (2nd ed.). New York: Oxford University Press.

Teeple, Gary (2000). *Globalization and the Decline of Social Reform.* Aurora: Garamond Press.

The Secretariat. (1996). *Beyond 2000: The new social policy agenda, socio-economic change and social policy.* Paris: OECD Head of Publications Service. (OECD/GD(96)170)

Titmus, R. (1976). *Commitment to welfare.* London: Allen & Unwin. Watts, R. (1989). Executive federalism: The comparative perspective. In D. Shugarman, & R. Whitaker (Eds), *Federalism and political community* (440). Peterborough, ON: Broadview Press.

Webber, M. (1998, May). *Measuring low income and poverty in Canada: An update.* Statistics Canada (cat. no. 98–13).

Wiegers, W. (2002, June). *The framing of poverty as "child poverty" and its implications for women.* Government of Canada (cat. no. SW21–94/2002E–IN).

Willms, J. D. (Ed.). (2002). *Vulnerable children: Findings from Canada's National Longitudinal Survey of children and youth.* Edmonton: University of Alberta Press.

Yelaja, S. (Ed.). (1978). *Canadian social policy.* Waterloo: Wilfrid Laurier University Press.

Yelaja, S. (1978). Canadian social policy: Perspectives. In Yelaja, S. (Ed.), *Canadian Social Policy* (1–26). Waterloo: Wilfrid Laurier University Press.